ANIMAL-INSPIRED MEALS and SNACKS FOR KIDS

40 EASY RECIPES THAT MAKE EATING FUN

Jill Mills

Skyhorse Publishing

For Von, Dane, and Levi, who have filled my kitchen
with crazy amounts of fun and my life with pure joy. I love you.

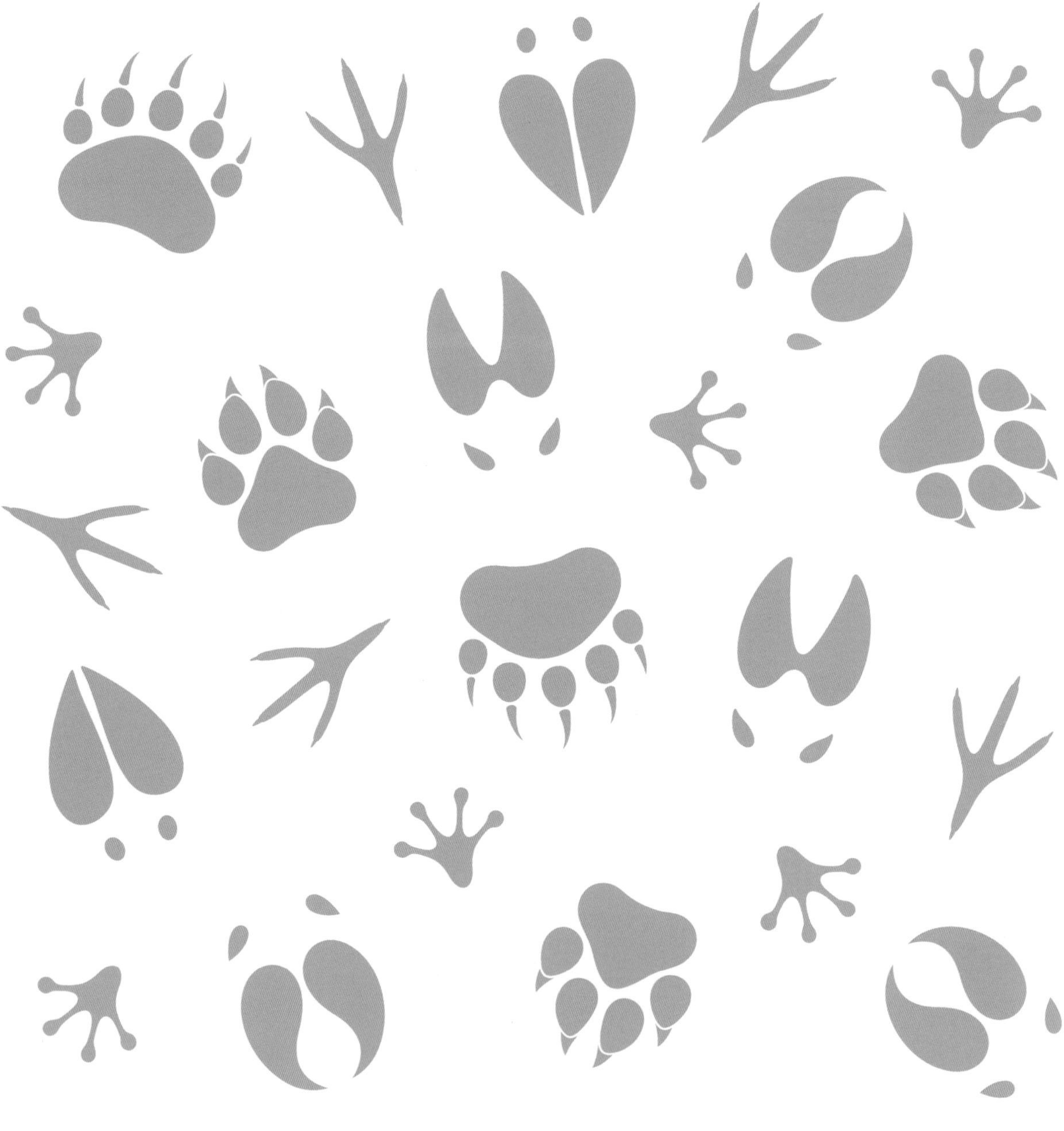

CONTENTS

INTRODUCTION

Years ago when my second son was a toddler, I was trying to come up with creative ways to get him to try new foods. He was such a picky eater and refused to try any fruits or vegetables. I decided to start turning his food into animals, characters, and other fun shapes to get him interested in eating healthy foods and trying new textures. I would also seek his input in coming up with fun food ideas, and he would be so proud of what he made. This opened up a whole new world of eating for him and got him to try just about anything!

Kids are so different in what foods they will try and stay away from because of taste or texture. There are some things that would never work with my boys no matter what it looks like; for example, kale. No matter what cute creation I try to make with kale, they are not going to go near it, but I still sneak a bit of it in a cute smoothie and they never know. I try to focus on foods that are practical—things that I know, based on my experience with my boys, picky eaters will really consider trying. However, we do not focus only on healthy food ideas. We also love creating themed treats for birthday parties, fun desserts to eat at home, and easy-to-make goodies for class parties.

When we began creating these fun treats on a regular basis and the word began to spread, my friends suggested that I start a blog to share our latest creations. At the time I had never even followed a blog and didn't know anything about it. I remember saying, "What is a blog?" (Yes, I was one of those I-don't-know–anything-about-computers people.)

Ultimately, I decided to start our *Kitchen Fun With My 3 Sons* blog to show friends and family our cute food ideas and party concepts that we had created. I really had no idea what I was doing, but just learned along the way. I never even considered sharing our ideas with the public, because I didn't think that anyone would be interested. The first time I submitted one of our fun food ideas was to an edible-craft site that my friend Meaghan Mountford (TheDecoratedCookie. com) used to contribute to. I was thinking, "There is no way that this will be shared." But I submitted it anyway. I remember being shocked when we noticed that our creation was on a well-known site, and my boys were so excited. That in itself gave us the confidence that others might be interested in re-creating our fun food ideas for their picky eaters and for parties. Our site became quite popular just shortly after that one share! I never dreamed that our blog would turn into what it is today and that our ideas would be loved by so many.

I created the blog with my boys' input in every part of it, and we have had so much fun with it these past four years. It has also been extremely rewarding to get weekly emails from our readers who have re-created our ideas and have also had success with getting their picky eaters to try new and healthy foods.

There are some people who wonder why we would take the time creating fun ideas with food. The way I look at it, your kids are only young once, and it goes by way too fast. Creating with food is like doing any other crafts with kids, and it's so amazing to see what these young imaginations can come up with. My boys have always blown me away with their creativity, and they have developed lots of our fun food ideas for our blog. I could never do any of this without them. You do not have to think of yourself as being an artist in order to create with food. I have absolutely no artistic background, but they have come up with almost one thousand original fun food ideas on our blog and for well-known name brands. Just know that if I can do it, you can definitely do it as well!

Some people have expressed concern about the time commitment involved in this kind of endeavor. I work a part-time job along with managing our blog and raising three boys with my husband, so I know better than anyone about not having a lot of time for extra activities like making fun food. However, the good news is that it doesn't take that much more time to add on a face or other fun details to a snack, lunch, or dinner. It's especially worthwhile if you have picky eaters or just want to create some fun memories with your kids. I try to come up with easy and simple ideas so that we (myself included) will not have to spend a lot of time making them. Also, I like to make things easy enough to enable the kids to create something all by themselves, or with just a little help. This not only will get the kids excited about making edible crafts, but it will also encourage them to make their own recipes.

I love to come up with fun treat ideas as well. Most kids will always love any treat no matter what it looks like, but there is something extra special about turning treats into a fun animal or character. I just love to see my boys' faces when I hand them not just a cake pop, but a monkey cake pop. Fun treats are also great for parties at home and class parties at school. Though some schools do not allow you to bring in your own treats, I feel very fortunate that my boys' school lets the parents bring in their own snacks and goodies to hand out to kids. I love getting stopped in my boys' school by other kids talking with me about their favorite memories of a fun party we had or a specific fun food idea that we created in the past. It puts a big smile on my face to know that those kids will have those fun memories, and that I had a part in that.

Once you familiarize yourself with the technique of creating fun food ideas, I'd also encourage you to start to make your own cakes and fun party food for your child's birthday parties. I know firsthand how hard it can be to find time in our busy schedules for things like that, but you might be surprised at how much your kids will appreciate your taking the time to make something unique just for them. Some of my favorite birthday memories as a child were the special cakes that my mom would make for me. You don't have to be super elaborate to make your treats or cake look extra cute. Most kids will not care about all the super fancy details on a cake or treat. Sometimes simple is just better, and you do not have to be a good baker or artist to create a fun cake or treat.

In the end, this book is all about spending time with your kids. It's about creating together, laughing together, making messes together, learning together, making memories, and having lots of kitchen fun with some wild recipes that your kids will love!

KIDS IN THE KITCHEN

Having your kids in the kitchen is not only a great way to spend time together, but it's also a great way to teach them about nutrition, basic math, following directions, colors, shapes, and creativity. As most of you know, it can be a bit messy, having little hands stirring, pouring, and taste testing, of course. However, those messy moments in which flour gets tossed around or beaters are licked can also create some awesome memories.

Having toddlers in the kitchen really helps teach them simple skills, starting with basic math. They love to count fruit slices, chocolate chips, pretzel sticks, or whatever kind of food is put in front of them. We used to use sorting sprinkles as a way for my youngest to learn his colors. They can also learn hand coordination when pouring ingredients, stirring, squeezing bags, and finger painting in flour. The importance of cleaning up your kitchen mess is another great lesson for them. These all sound like very simple things, but they are all a part of learning.

For the kids who are a bit older, they can learn about measurements, time, reading, following directions, cleaning up, and creativity. I know that with my boys, I like to let them figure out the measurements and times. For example, I ask them to tell me how long it will take to cook or bake something according to the directions. They will keep track of the time. I also have them pour ingredients in measuring cups on their own to follow the directions of a recipe. Seeing the measuring cups helps them to visually understand why ¼ cup is smaller than ¾ cup.

The best part of having the kids in the kitchen is that I am able to witness, firsthand, their creativity. My boys always amaze me with what they come up with. My eleven-year-old is an artist and has come up with lots of the

creations that we have shared on our blog. He has such a good eye—he has had me change things up often before we share a photo online, and it's always so much better the way he sees it. My eight-year-old likes to be more hands-on with the cooking as opposed to the decorating. He likes to toss in a little of this and a little of that and is adventurous with food. My four-year-old likes to get his hands on and in everything, along with being our best taste tester. He had an awful femur break when he was three and was in a body cast for six long weeks. It was so hard to see him having to stay put on a pillow in that cast for weeks. However, he would pull and drag himself, using his elbows, into the kitchen when he would hear me cooking. He has always loved to be in the kitchen. It would bring me to tears seeing him trying so hard to come and help me stir whatever I was making.

Having the kids help you with meals is also a great way to get them to try new foods. My eight-year-old was such a picky eater, but having him help make the recipes himself made him feel so proud. He even tried the recipes he created. Making the recipes look fun also really helped—but at one point he didn't want to try anything unless it looked "cute." This was fine with me, as long as it got him to eat healthy foods. Those of you with picky eaters will understand how frustrating it is when your kids will not try anything. Of course, there are those who might think it is a parent's fault because their kids should eat whatever they serve them. However, that is just not true. I have three boys, parented the same way, and they are all very different. It just really depends on the child. It is also important not to give up on finding ways to add nutrition in your kid's diet.

We are living in a time where there is a huge amount of processed foods in our grocery stores. This is contributing to obesity in children. It's so easy to grab the boxed items for a quick dinner for those of us with busy schedules, and I am also guilty of this myself. Kids are such a target for brands that make unhealthy processed foods. It is our job as parents to keep them educated about what is in their food. This is why it is important for us to talk with our kids about why healthy food choices are essential for our diet. Yes, it can take a little more time to prepare, but this is why creating fun food ideas makes being in the kitchen much more exciting for kids. I personally see nothing wrong with creating and letting the kids eat treats from time to time, as long as it is in moderation. I talk with my boys often about this subject. If they want a treat, I will gladly allow it, as long as they run around and play outside for a longer period of time. We all love treats in my house, and I find nothing wrong with that as long we are including healthy choices in our diet and exercising. It is all about balance.

There are lots of kid-friendly cooking supplies that are available. This also makes a child feel like a little chef. Let them plan a breakfast, lunch, or dinner and keep their kid-friendly kitchen tools in a special place. For other tools, kids will need your assistance. For example, children should be supervised when handling toothpicks (make sure they remove them from the foods before eating!), and adults should take the reins when it comes to using sharp knives and oven use.

My boys have even created menus to choose from, seating me at their very own restaurant. Kids also love having their own special apron and it makes them feel in charge. My boys have hot rod aprons that they think are awesome, and they really put me to work when they put those aprons on.

All of these things can be very beneficial in many ways. Maybe one day they will have their own cooking show or become a top chef. However, for me the best part is all of the wonderful memories we are creating together.

Part I

Breakfast

Chicken and Egg Breakfast

This fun Chicken and Egg Breakfast includes pancakes, eggs, granola, fruit, and bacon. Kids will get a kick out of this, especially those of you who have backyard chickens. You will be surprised at how easy this is to make, and I guarantee a big smile on those little faces when the kids sit down to eat this fun breakfast.

Ingredients

- ¾ cup all-purpose flour
- 2 teaspoons baking powder
- ½ teaspoon salt
- ½ tablespoon white sugar
- ¾ cup milk
- 1 egg, beaten
- 1 ½ tablespoons butter, melted
- 1 strawberry
- 1 orange slice
- 1 piece of turkey bacon (cooked)
- 1 chocolate chip
- granola
- 1 hard-boiled egg

Directions
• • • • • •

1 In a large mixing bowl mix together the flour, baking powder, salt, and sugar. Create a well in the center and pour in the milk, egg, and butter.

2 Lightly spray a large pan with cooking spray. Pour the pancake batter in the pan over low heat into a large pancake. Lightly brown on both sides and place the pancake on a plate. Cut around the edges in the shape of a chicken using kitchen scissors.

3 Cut out the tail and wings from the scraps and place them on the pancake chicken body. Cut a strawberry into slices and place the slices on top of the head. Cut an orange slice in half using a knife and place it on the front to look like a beak. Place a small piece of a strawberry slice under the orange beak for the wattle.

4 Cut off slices of the cooked turkey bacon using kitchen scissors and place the slices on the bottom for the chicken feet. Place a chocolate chip on the side for the eye. Spread granola around the bottom of the chicken pancake to look like bedding. Place the hard-boiled egg on the granola to look like the chicken just laid an egg.

Tips and Tricks

You can use pancake mix in place of the recipe. You can use cereal in place of the granola. You can use strawberries cut into strips for the legs and feet instead of bacon. You can cut out the wing using a heart-shaped cookie cutter.

Animal Fact

A female chicken is called a hen and a male chicken is called a rooster. A chicken has a comb on the head and two wattles under the neck. The male has a larger comb compared to the female. The male makes a cock-a-doodle-doo sound, and the hen makes a cluck-cluck sound. There are over 25 billion chickens in the world, which makes them the most popular kind of bird. Chickens eat worms, insects, seeds, grains, snails, slugs, fruits, vegetables, and many other kinds of food. A hen can lay more than 300 eggs a year! Chicken eggs come in different colors like white, brown, blue, or pink. Chickens love to play and make great pets.

Whole Wheat Walrus Waffles

This walrus is so easy to decorate and this whole wheat waffle recipe is a favorite in our house. I am sure your kids will think this is pretty awesome, as my boys did!

Ingredients

- 2 large eggs
- 1 ¾ cups milk
- ¼ cup oil (or melted butter)
- 2 tablespoons honey
- 1 teaspoon ground cinnamon
- ¼ teaspoon baking soda
- 1 ½ cups whole wheat flour
- 1 teaspoon baking powder
- ⅛ teaspoon salt
- cooking spray or butter
- 2 pieces of turkey bacon (cooked)
- 1 banana
- 3 blueberries

Directions

• • • • • •

1 Preheat your waffle iron.

2 In a large mixing bowl whisk together the eggs, milk, oil, honey, cinnamon, and baking soda until well combined. Add in the flour, baking powder, and salt and whisk together just until the large lumps disappear.

3 When the waffle iron is hot, dab it with a little butter or spray with cooking spray. Spoon some of the batter onto the center of the iron. Cook on your preferred setting.

4 Keep the waffles warm by covering with aluminum foil until you finish cooking all of them. Place one waffle on a plate. Cut 2 slices from a banana. Place the slices on the top of the waffle for the eyes. Add blueberries on top of the banana slices to look like pupils. Add another blueberry underneath for the nose. Cut the rest of the banana in half lengthwise and place the halves under the nose to look like tusks. Add the cooked bacon over the bananas to look like a mustache.

Tips and Tricks

Follow the instructions that came with your waffle maker to know how long they should be cooked. Ours has a light setting to indicate light, medium, and dark. You can also spray on whipped cream or cut apple slices for the teeth if you do not have a banana. You can use raisins in place of the blueberries for the eyes and nose.

Animal Fact

Walruses are mostly found near the Arctic Circle hanging out with hundreds of their companions. They are known for their long white tusks, mustaches, flat flippers, and large flabby bodies. Both males and females have two large tusks that are used for defense, getting out of water, and cutting through ice. The tusks can be more than three feet long on males. A male walrus can weigh over 3,000 pounds! A walrus's favorite food is shellfish. Even though walruses are so large with huge tusks, they are known to be the gentle giants of the Arctic.

Birdy Breakfast

This Birdy Breakfast includes pancakes, eggs, hash browns, and fruit. This is a fun breakfast to make during the spring. If your kids do not like hard-boiled eggs, you can scramble the eggs and shape them into the baby birds.

Ingredients

- ¾ cup all-purpose flour
- 2 teaspoons baking powder
- ½ teaspoon salt
- ½ tablespoon white sugar
- ¾ cup milk
- 1 egg, beaten
- 1 ½ tablespoons butter, melted
- frozen hash browns
- 1 hard-boiled egg
- 1 slice of cheddar cheese
- 1 raisin
- green grapes

Directions
• • • • • •

1 In a large mixing bowl, mix together the flour, baking powder, salt, and sugar. Create a well in the center and pour in the milk, egg, and butter.

2 Lightly spray a large pan with cooking spray. Pour the pancake batter in the pan over low heat in the shape of a tree with one large branch. Lightly brown on both sides and place the pancake on a plate.

3 Scoop out a handful of frozen hash browns and fry them in a pan according to the package directions. Place the cooked hash browns on top of the branch to look like a nest. Cut the hard-boiled egg in half and place the 2 halves on top of the hash browns. Cut out little wings, hair, and a beak from the slice of cheddar cheese and place them on top of the eggs.

4 Cut pieces of a raisin to make the eyes. Cut green grapes in half using kitchen scissors. Place the grape halves on the end of the branch to look like leaves.

Tips and Tricks

You can use premade pancake mix in place of the recipe. You can use strips of bacon for the nest instead of the hash browns. Slices of kiwi can be replaced for the grapes. You can cut a strawberry in half for the birds to replace the egg.

Animal Fact

There are around 10,000 different bird species around the world. The smallest in size is the bee hummingbird, which is 2.24 inches in total length (including the tip of the beak and tail). The largest bird in the world is the ostrich, which can get up to nine feet tall! Most birds survive on a diet of insect and plants such as fruits, nuts, berries, and seeds. Many birds are kept as pets, including parakeets, lovebirds, canaries, and parrots.

Cinnamon Bunny Buns

Bunnies are so cute to create out of food, and these bunny buns take just minutes to make. The kids will not even notice that you use very little icing because of how adorable these bunnies look. This is also a fun breakfast to make the kids on Easter morning, served with their colored Easter eggs.

Ingredients

- 1 package of large cinnamon rolls
- 2 slices of turkey bacon (cooked)
- 1 strawberry
- raisins
- marshmallow bits

Directions

1 Preheat the oven to 350 degrees F.

2 Open the package of large cinnamon rolls. Pull off 1 cinnamon roll and unroll it. Cut the strip in half. Roll the other half back up with the cinnamon on the inside. Lay the other half on top with the sides hanging down.

3 Cut the ends at a point using kitchen scissors to look like ears. Bake for 20 minutes or until the buns are lightly browned.

4 Cut the pieces of turkey bacon into thin slices using kitchen scissors. Cut three holes on each side of the buns using a knife and press in the turkey bacon strips for whiskers.

5 Take your strawberry and cut thin slices using a knife. Cut the slices into the shape of a nose and place them on top of the cinnamon buns. Snip off the corner of the icing that came with the cinnamon roll package and squeeze on two eyes. Place one raisin on the icing for each pupil.

6 Cut raisins in half and line them up under the strawberry nose to look like a mouth. Cut the marshmallow bits in half to look like teeth and place them below the mouth.

Tips and Tricks

You can use any cinnamon roll recipe for this in place of the premade package of cinnamon rolls. You can use mini chocolate chips in place of the raisins. If you do not have strawberries, you can cut out a nose from the turkey bacon. You can also make the ears stand up and add a little of the white icing in the center of the ears for a different look.

Animal Fact

Most rabbits are small, but rabbits such as the jackrabbit can grow up to two feet in size! Rabbits are herbivores, which means that they have a plant-based diet and do not eat any meats. During the warm months rabbits like to eat grasses, herbs, peas, lettuce, and greens. In the winter months they like to eat twigs, bark, and buds. Rabbits like to come out at dusk and dawn to find food. The low light helps them to hide from predators. Rabbits breed three to four times every year and produce three to eight babies each time. Wild rabbits create their own homes by tunneling in the ground.

Doggy Oatmeal

Oatmeal is a great breakfast for kids and is a healthy way to really fill them up. However, my boys have never been big fans of oatmeal. This is a recipe that they really like and is very easy to decorate. This is also a great way to add some fruits to their breakfast that they normally would never eat.

Ingredients

- 1 ½ cups milk
- ½ cup quick cooking oats
- 2 tablespoons white sugar
- ½ teaspoon ground cinnamon
- ⅛ teaspoon salt
- 2 strawberries
- 2 blueberries
- 3 raisins
- 1 banana

Directions

• • • • • •

1 Combine the milk, quick cooking oats, sugar, cinnamon, and salt in a saucepan over medium heat. Bring to a boil, stirring constantly for about two minutes.

2 Remove from heat and spoon the oatmeal into bowls. Cut a strawberry in half and place on the top sides to look like ears. Cut the other strawberry into slices. Add a slice on the top right side for the eye and another small slice for the nose. Add blueberries for the eyes. Cut the raisins in half and make the mouth. Cut a little piece from the strawberry to make a tongue.

3 Cut four slices from a banana and then cut the banana in half. Place the banana half on the plate under the oatmeal. Place two slices on each of the ends of the banana half to look like a dog bone.

Tips and Tricks

You can use honey instead of sugar and add nutmeg for more flavor. You can use chocolate chips instead of the blueberries. You can also substitute instant oatmeal for this recipe.

Animal Fact

The domestic dog has been one of the most popular companions to humans for the past 10,000 years. There are hundreds of different breeds of dogs, with the most popular being the Labrador. Domestic dogs share many behaviors with their wild relatives, including marking their territories and burying bones for future use. One of the largest dogs is the Great Dane, which has a height up to 34 inches and weight from 100 to 200 pounds! One of the smallest dogs is a Chihuahua. The smallest Chihuahua on record measures 3.8 inches tall. Domestic dogs are omnivores and eat a variety of foods including grains, vegetables, and meats.

Kangaroo Pancakes

There is something so cute about kangaroos, unless they decide to start punching you. My boys have always loved seeing how baby kangaroos are carried in their mommy's pouch and how they hop around. These fun kangaroo pancakes are a great way to start talking about all of the unique things about kangaroos.

Ingredients

- ¾ cups all-purpose flour
- 2 teaspoons baking powder
- ½ teaspoon salt
- ½ tablespoon white sugar
- ¾ cup milk
- 1 egg, beaten
- 1 ½ tablespoons butter, melted
- 1 tablespoon cocoa
- 1 mini marshmallow
- 9 chocolate chips
- 9 mini chocolate chips

Directions

1 In a large mixing bowl, mix together the flour, baking powder, salt, and sugar. Create a well in the center and pour in the milk, egg, and butter. Mix well. Save about a half cup of pancake mixture for later use. Then mix the cocoa into the main mixture.

2 Lightly spray a large pan with cooking spray. Pour the pancake mix as one large pancake in the pan over low heat. Lightly brown on both sides and place the pancake on a plate. Do the same with the rest of the pancake batter; make a smaller pancake and place that above the large pancake on the plate.

3 Make another large pancake and cut it in half. Cut out four small circles, two ears, and a tail from one of the pancake halves using kitchen scissors. Cut out the other pancake half to fit on top of the large pancake on the plate to look like a pouch.

4 Make a small pancake with your reserved pancake batter without the cocoa. Cut out that small pancake into a baby kangaroo using your kitchen scissors.

5 Cut a marshmallow in half and place the halves on the top pancake for the eyes. Place three chocolate chips on each foot and three mini chocolate chips on each hand. Add two chocolate chips on each eye for the pupils. Place a chocolate chip under the eyes for the nose. Place mini chocolate chips on the face of the baby kangaroo.

Tips and Tricks

You can replace the pancake recipe with pancake mix. You can use raisins in place of the chocolate chips. Small round cookie cutters work great to cut out the feet and hands. You can also use large round cookie cutters to cut out the head and body. You can replace the marshmallows with two banana slices.

Animal Fact

Kangaroos are found in Australia and possess powerful hind legs, a long, strong tail, and small front legs. A newborn kangaroo is called a joey, which is about the size of a small grape when it is born. When the baby joey is born, the mom keeps it safe in her pouch. Kangaroos are herbivores and like to eat grasses, flowers, leaves, moss, and even insects. The largest breed is the Red Kangaroo, which can reach speeds of 35 miles an hour. They can also cover 25 feet in a single leap and can jump 6 feet high! Kangaroos are known to box each other in defense and can also bite. A kangaroo can live around six years in the wild and up to 20 years in captivity.

Owl Breakfast

This cute owl makes a complete breakfast of pancakes, eggs, fruit, and bacon. This is a fun breakfast to make, and your kids will think it is a real hoot!

Ingredients

- ¾ cup all-purpose flour
- 2 teaspoons baking powder
- ½ teaspoon salt
- ½ tablespoon white sugar
- ¾ cup milk
- 1 egg, beaten
- 1 ½ tablespoons butter, melted

- 1 hard-boiled egg
- 1 black grape
- 1 piece of cooked turkey bacon
- 1 clementine
- 4 green grapes
- 4 strawberries

Directions

• • • • • •

1 In a large mixing bowl, mix together the flour, baking powder, salt, and sugar. Create a well in the center and pour in the milk, egg, and butter.

2 Lightly spray a large pan with cooking spray. Pour the pancake batter in the pan over low heat, making a large pancake. Lightly brown both sides of the pancake. Cut around the edges using kitchen scissors into an oval to fit on your plate. Place the pancake on a plate and save the scraps. Cut out the two ears from your scraps and place them on the top sides of the head.

3 Peel and cut your hard-boiled egg in half using a knife. Place the egg halves on top of the pancake to look like eyes with the yolk showing. Cut the black grape in half and place the halves on top of the eggs to look like pupils.

4 Place the piece of turkey bacon on the bottom of the owl pancake. Cut slices of clementine to make the beak and feet. Cut green grapes in half and place them on the end of the turkey bacon to look like leaves. Cut the strawberries into slices and place them on the sides of the pancake to look like wings. Use some of the strawberry scraps for the top to look like hair.

Tips and Tricks

You can use pancake mix in place of the pancake recipe. You can use an orange or cheddar cheese for the beak and feet. You can use white cheese or whipped cream to make the eyes in place of the egg. You can use a blueberry or raisins instead of the black grape. You can use slices of kiwi in place of the green grapes.

Animal Fact

Owls can twist their necks almost completely around to turn their heads without moving their shoulders. They do this because they do not have regular eyeballs, and this is the way they can see around them. Owls' eyes are long and shaped like a tube, which means their eyes cannot turn in their sockets. Even though owls have big eyes with great vision, they actually use their excellent hearing to hunt for prey by sound. Most owls have feather tufts on the tops of their heads that are commonly mistaken for ears. Their ears are located on the sides of their head.

Pink Piggy Smoothie and Bagel Breakfast

Smoothies are a great way to load your kids up on fruit in the mornings for breakfast, especially if the smoothie looks like a cute pig! This is such an easy breakfast to make, and the kids will love it!

Smoothie Ingredients

- 1 banana, peeled
- 2 cups of frozen strawberries
- 12 ounces strawberry yogurt
- 1 strawberry
- 2 chocolate chips
- 2 mini chocolate chips

Smoothie Directions

1. Blend the banana, frozen strawberries, and strawberry yogurt in a blender or juicer. Pour the strawberry smoothie into a small glass. Cut the top off of a strawberry. Cut off one slice and add that on top of the smoothie. Cut another slice of the strawberry and then cut that slice in half. Place the strawberry halves on the top sides to look like ears. Place two chocolate chips on top for the eyes and two mini chocolate chips on the strawberry half to look like a pig's nose.

Bagel Ingredients

- 1 bagel half
- strawberry cream cheese
- 1 strawberry
- 2 chocolate chips
- 2 mini chocolate chips

Bagel Directions

1 Toast the bagel half and place it on a plate. Spread strawberry cream cheese on top. Cut the strawberry into slices. Place one strawberry slice on top of the bagel (around the middle). Cut another slice in half and place that on the top sides for ears. Place two mini chocolate chips on top of the strawberry half to look like a pig's nose. Place two chocolate chips above the nose, for the eyes.

Tips and Tricks

You can make any smoothie recipe that turns out a pink color using strawberries, raspberries, or cherries. If you do not have strawberry cream cheese, you can mix a little bit of strawberry jam with regular cream cheese for a nice pink color.

Animal Fact

Pigs have a reputation of being very dirty, but they are actually very clean animals. This reputation comes from seeing pigs rolling around in mud to stay cool in warm environments, but pigs that live in cool environments stay very clean. Pigs are also very intelligent and have a great sense of smell. Pigs are one of the smartest of all domesticated animals and are known to be smarter than dogs! Some people like to keep pigs as pets.

Part II

Lunch

Panda Pita Pizza

Kids love to create their very own pizza that is the perfect size for them, and this Panda Pizza is really easy to make. Let them get creative and make any animal or character they like, using an assortment of meats and veggies. It will be a huge hit with the kids!

Ingredients

(makes 2)
- 2 pitas
- ½ cup pizza sauce
- 1 cup shredded mozzarella cheese

- 10 turkey pepperoni slices
- 1 slice of provolone cheese
- 1 black olive

Directions

● ● ● ● ● ●

1 Preheat the oven to 350 degrees F. Place the pitas on a baking sheet. Spread ¼ cup of pizza sauce on each pita. Place two pepperoni slices on the top sides for ears. Sprinkle ½ cup of shredded mozzarella cheese on each pita, covering the edge of the pepperoni that is touching the sauce.

2 Place two pepperoni slices on top of the shredded cheese for the eyes. Using kitchen scissors, cut out another pepperoni slice into a nose and mouth. Place the pitas in the oven for 10 to 15 minutes, until the cheese is melted.

3 Cut out two small circles from the slice of provolone cheese and place them on top of the pepperoni eyes. Using a knife, cut out two very small dots from the black olive and place them on the cheese eyes to look like pupils. Place the pitas on a plate and serve.

Tips and Tricks

You can also make these by flattening out premade biscuits using your fingers or rolling them out with a dough roller. Add the pizza sauce, cheese, and pepperoni. Bake them as directed on the package. Then add your provolone cheese cutouts and olives. You can also make a large panda pizza by stacking the pepperoni slices and shaping them into the ears, eyes, nose, and mouth.

Animal Fact

Wild pandas live in mountainous regions of China. Pandas are an endangered species, and there are only about 1,000 left in the world. Pandas love to eat bamboo and are known to be great climbers. They also have a highly developed sense of smell. Baby pandas are born a solid white and develop their coloring later. Pandas have a life span of around 20 years. Pandas are one of the most popular zoo animals because of how rare and adorable they are!

Cow Lunch

There is something about cows that kids just love. Maybe it's their *moo* sounds or their laziness. You will be surprised at how simple it is to create this fun cow lunch, and this is also a great way to get your picky eaters to eat some healthy foods for lunch.

Ingredients

- 2 pieces of whole grain bread
- 2 slices of provolone cheese
- 1 slice of turkey
- raisins
- 2 black grapes
- 1 small yellow bell pepper
- lettuce

Directions
• • • • • •

1 Cut both of the pieces of whole grain bread into circles, making one of them just a bit smaller than the other. Make sure to save the scraps. Place the bread on a plate.

2 Place the cheese on the bread and cut the edges to fit on top using kitchen scissors. Cut the slice of turkey to look like a nose and place it on top of the cheese for the head. Cut two ears from the bread scraps and place them on the top sides of the head. Cut pieces of the cheese scraps to fit on top of the ears and do the same with the sliced turkey.

3 Place different-sized raisins on the body to look like spots. Cut a large raisin in half for the eyes and a small raisin in half for the nose. Line up raisins in the back for the tail and around the neck for the collar.

4 Cut a triangle shape from the small yellow bell pepper and place it on the raisin collar to look like a bell. Cut slits on a lettuce leaf using kitchen scissors and place it on the bottom of the plate to look like grass. Cut two small legs using the bread scraps. Place two black grapes on the legs, for the feet.

Tips and Tricks

You can make any type of sandwich that your child prefers, such as PB&J or any other meat fillings. You can replace the lettuce with green grapes. You can use ham instead of turkey.

Animal Fact

There are over 1 billion cattle in the world. The average life span of a cow is between 15 and 20 years. An average cow weighs about 1,200 pounds. Most dairy cows can produce up to six and a half gallons of milk per day! Cows only have teeth on the bottom of their mouth and like to eat hay, silage, and grass. You will find cows roaming the streets of India, where they are considered sacred.

Horsey Hot Dogs

Hot dogs are always a favorite with kids, and they will fall in love with these Horsey Hot Dogs. This is such an easy lunch to make. Let the kids get creative with extra pretzel rods to add a body and legs. These would also be really cute to serve at a horse-themed party.

Ingredients

- 1 package of crescent rounds
- hot dogs
- pretzel rods
- ketchup
- 1 raisin
- pretzel sticks

Directions

• • • • • •

1 Preheat the oven according to the directions on the crescent rounds package. Unroll the crescent rounds into strips. Cut the hot dog at an angle in the middle. Rotate one of the hot dog halves and re-connect it to the other half, creating an L shape. Wrap one of the crescent strips around each hot dog half, holding them together tightly and leaving an end of both hot dog halves exposed.

2 Place the wrapped hot dogs on a baking pan and cook according to the directions on the crescent rounds package. When the hot dogs are done baking, cut a hole in the bottom of the hot dog using a knife. Break the pretzel rods in half and push a pretzel rod half into the hole.

3 Squeeze on a little ketchup on the side of the hot dog to look like reins. You can also add the ketchup using a toothpick. Cut pieces from a raisin and add them on for the eye and nose. Stick pretzel sticks into the top of the hot dog to look like horsehair.

Tips and Tricks

You can also add cheese on the hot dog before wrapping it with the crescent dough. Sliced cheese can be shaped into hair in place of the pretzel sticks. You can also use a corn dog, in place of a hot dog, by taking it off the stick. Follow the same directions and replace the stick with the pretzel rod.

Animal Fact

Horses have had a long relationship with humans and were once a major form of transportation. There are over 350 breeds of horses that come in a number of sizes, colors, and skill sets. A male horse is called a stallion and a female horse is called a mare. Horses are grazing animals and mostly eat hay and grasses. Horses can sleep standing up or lying down, and they also have the largest eyes of any other land mammal.

Pigs in a Snail Shell

This is our version of pigs in a blanket. The kids will get a kick out of these silly snails on their plate for lunch.

Ingredients

- 1 package of turkey hot dogs
- 1 package of crescent dough
- 1 slice of provolone cheese
- pretzel sticks
- raisins

Directions
• • • • • •

1 Preheat the oven to 375 degrees F. Open the hot dog package and place the hot dogs on a work surface. Starting in the middle of the hot dog, cut slits into one half of the hot dog, making sure not to cut all the way through. Leave the other half of the hot dog uncut.

2 Open the package of crescent dough. Cut each of the crescents into three strips and press two of the strips together at the ends, forming one long strip out of each crescent roll. Start wrapping the hot dog with the long crescent strip in the middle of the hot dog, working down the sliced side to the end (leaving extra crescent to work with).

3 Bend the covered hot dog around to the center (the reason you cut the slits) to form a circle. Take the extra crescent strip and wrap it around the middle of the hot dog to secure. Then wrap the rest of your crescent strip around the top, forming a spiral circle to look like a shell. Do the same with the other hot dogs and long strips of crescent dough.

4 Bake for 10 to 15 minutes or until the snail hot dogs are lightly browned. Cut out two small circles from a slice of provolone cheese and place one on each side of the hot dog for the eyes. Break pretzel sticks in half and press two into the tops of each hot dog for antennas. Cut small pieces of raisin and place the pieces on the cheese eyes for pupils.

Tips and Tricks

You can use any kind of hot dogs. Crescent rounds will also work well with this, in lieu of the crescent dough. Roll them out and do not cut them into strips. Wrap them the same as directed.

Animal Fact

Snails belong to a group of mollusks known as gastropods. Snails are nocturnal and are most likely to come out at night or very early in the morning. Snails cannot hear. To find food they use their sense of smell. Some snails hibernate in the colder months. They cover their bodies with a thin layer of mucus to help prevent them from drying out. There are large snails and very small snails. One of the largest snails is the Giant African Land Snail, averaging 8 inches in size. Other smaller snail species measure only a few centimeters long as adults and weigh just a couple of ounces.

Crabwiches

I created these crab sandwiches to get my boys to try tuna salad for the first time. They refused to even take a bite of tuna until these cute crabs showed up on their plate. They not only ate them, but ended up loving tuna fish! You can always use any filling to make this, but a seafood filling just seems fitting for this fun lunch.

Ingredients

- 1 (6-ounce) can tuna, drained
- ¼ cup of chopped celery
- ½ cup mayonnaise
- ½ teaspoon of lemon juice
- 1 tablespoon chopped fresh parsley
- ¼ teaspoon garlic powder
- ¼ teaspoon onion powder
- ⅛ teaspoon salt
- pinch of black pepper
- croissants
- 1 red apple
- 2 raisins
- toothpicks

Directions
• • • • • • •

1 In a large bowl, combine the tuna, chopped celery, mayonnaise, lemon juice, parsley, garlic powder, onion powder, salt, and pepper. Mix well.

2 Cut the croissants in half using a knife. Spread the tuna salad on the bottom of the croissant half and place the other croissant half on top. Place the filled croissant on a plate.

3 Cut the red apple in half using a knife. Cut that apple half in half again. Using a knife, shape those apple pieces into claws to fit the croissants at the point.

4 Take the other apple half and cut a large slice. Cut two circles (without the peel) out of the apple slice. Attach the apple circles to a toothpick and place them on top of the croissant to look like eyes. Cut a raisin in half and press the cut sides on the front of the apple eyes for pupils (they will stick).

Tips and Tricks

You can make any filling for this sandwich, including egg salad or different meats and cheeses. You can replace the apple using a pear. You can change out the raisins for chocolate chips.

Animal Fact

There are over 6,000 species of crab found in the oceans, fresh waters, and land around the world. There are very tiny crabs and very large crabs. Most crabs have flat bodies that allow them to squeeze into very narrow crevices. Crabs like to eat both plants and animals, which makes them omnivores. Crabs have ten legs (two of them being their claws) and they walk sideways. An average life span of a crab is between one and three years.

Baby Birdy Egg Salad Lunch

This Baby Bird Egg Salad Lunch is a great way to get your picky eaters to try egg salad. My boys would never try egg salad because of the texture. This cute baby bird idea got them to try it for the first time, and they loved it!

Ingredients

- 2 hard-boiled eggs
- 2 tablespoons mayonnaise
- ½ teaspoon of spicy mustard
- salt and pepper to taste
- whole grain bread
- pretzel sticks
- 2 baby carrots
- 2 raisins

Directions
• • • • • •

1 Cut off the ends from one of the hard-boiled eggs before chopping and set aside. Make sure the rest of the first egg and the whole second egg are chopped up finely without any of the egg white showing. Combine the first four ingredients and blend well.

2 Cut both of the pieces of whole grain bread in a circle, leaving one of them a little bit smaller. Make sure to save the scraps. Place the round pieces of bread on a plate, one above the other. Spread the egg salad on top. Cut out two pieces of hair and two wings from the bread scraps and also top those with the egg salad, connecting the pieces by using the egg salad as an adhesive.

3 Place pretzel sticks on the bottom of the egg salad bird to look like a nest. Cut the two baby carrots in half and shape the halves into a beak and two feet, using a knife. Cut the reserved egg white slices in two circles using a knife and place them on the front for eyes. Place two raisins on the egg whites for the pupils.

Tips and Tricks

You can use a slice of white cheese for the eyes if you forget to reserve a piece of egg white. You can use a slice of cheddar cheese in place of the carrot.

Animal Fact

Mama birds build nests to help protect their babies in their eggs from weather and predators. Birds will use any available material such as leaves, sticks, mosses, feathers, or anything they can fly away with to build the nest. Adult birds almost always sit on the eggs to help keep them warm until they hatch. When baby birds are ready to hatch, they use their beaks to break open their hard-shelled eggs. Most baby birds eat insects to help them grow quickly.

Ladybug Lunch

This is a fun lunch to make in the spring, using a kid-friendly PB&J sandwich! This is also a great way to get the kids to eat lots of fruit for lunch. This idea would be really cute for a ladybug-themed party.

Ingredients

- 2 slices of whole wheat bread
- peanut butter
- strawberry jam
- 9 raisins
- 3 black grapes

- 4 strawberries
- 5 marshmallow bits
- black edible marker
- 12 mini chocolate chips
- 1 red toothpick

Directions

1. Cut out circles from your two slices of whole wheat bread using kitchen scissors. Cut out one slice and use that slice as a guide to cut out the other one. Spread peanut butter on one side of one slice of bread and place it on a plate. Cut a U shape out of the other slice and spread the strawberry jam on top of the rest of this slice (the "non-U" part). Place it on top of the peanut butter slices.

2 Place four raisins on each side of the jam-topped bread slice. Place a black grape at the front for the head.

3 Cut a small slice from the bottom of each strawberry and place the strawberries on the sides of the sandwich. Cut the tips off the other black grapes and place them on the ends of the strawberries for the little ladybug heads.

4 Cut the marshmallow bits in half and press them on the grape tips and the grape on the sandwich to look like eyes. Press a black edible marker in the middle of the marshmallow bits to make the pupils.

5 Cut a tiny slice from the strawberry scraps and press it on the black grape for a mouth. Press in the mini chocolate chips on the tops of the strawberries (about three chips per strawberry) to look like spots. Break a red toothpick in half. Cut off the tips from another raisin and press the raisin tips on the ends of the toothpicks. Poke the toothpicks in the top of the black grape for the antennas.

Tips and Tricks

You can use round cookie cutters to cut out the bread slices instead of using kitchen scissors. You can use strawberry jelly instead of jam, but jam does spread more evenly. You can use dates instead of black grapes. You can replace the raisins with regular chocolate chips.

Animal Fact

Ladybugs have tiny, spotted, oval-shaped domes with short legs and antennas. Their spots and colors are meant to make them unappealing to predators. Ladybugs can secrete fluids that give them a foul taste to protect them against predators. Farmers especially love ladybugs, because they save gardens by eating pest insects. Ladybugs on average live to be two to three years old.

Lion Burgers with Sweet Potato Fries

Your kids will be roaring with excitement when they get this fun Lion Burger for lunch! This is also how I get my boys to eat sweet potato fries instead of regular fries. It is so easy to make your own sweet potato fries, and with homemade fries, you actually know what your kids are eating. The Italian diced tomatoes make these burgers taste so good, and it's a great way to get your kids to eat tomatoes. Just make sure that you get the petite tomatoes, and they will never even notice.

Ingredients

Burgers

- 1 pound ground turkey
- 1 (14.5-ounce) can petite Italian diced tomatoes, drained very well
- 1 egg (beaten)
- ¼ cup bread crumbs
- ⅓ cup Parmesan cheese
- hamburger buns
- 1 slice of cheddar
- 1 slice of provolone cheese
- black olives
- pretzel sticks

Sweet potato fries

- sweet potatoes (one potato per burger)
- olive oil
- cornstarch
- salt and pepper to taste

Instructions for burgers

1 Combine the ground turkey, petite Italian diced tomatoes, beaten egg, bread crumbs, and Parmesan cheese. Form into patties and season with salt and pepper.

2 Place the patties on the grill or in a pan over medium heat. Cook on both sides until cooked through.

Instructions for sweet potato fries

1 Preheat the oven to 425 degrees F. Peel the sweet potatoes and cut them into small slices. Try to cut them into identical sizes. In a bowl or large plastic bag, toss your slices with 1 tablespoon of olive oil and a pinch of cornstarch for each potato you are using. Season with salt and pepper and toss to fully coat.

2 Pour the potato slices on a dark coated nonstick baking sheet (you can use any baking sheet, but the dark coated sheets work better for crispiness). Arrange your potato slices in a single layer, not overcrowding.

3 Bake for 15 minutes (for as many potatoes that you decide to use), and then, using a metal spatula, flip the slices so they can cook on all sides. Bake for 15 more minutes until the fries are crispy and lightly starting to brown. Be careful not to burn them.

Final prep instructions

1 Place the burger inside a hamburger bun and then place it on a plate. Arrange the sweet potato fries around the burger to look like the lion's mane. Cut out the ears using a slice of cheddar and a slice of provolone cheese. Cut out the eyes using the provolone cheese. Cut pieces of black olives to make the nose, mouth, pupils, and eyebrows. Press in the pretzel sticks on the sides of the bun to look like whiskers.

Tips and Tricks

You can use any kind of burger and also change out the types of cheeses. You can replace the black olives using raisins if your kids refuse to eat olives. You can replace the sweet potato fries using regular fries and the colors will still look good.

Animal Fact

Lions are often known as the "King of the Jungle" for their power, strength, and loud roars! Lions are very social animals and the only cats that live in groups, called prides. Lions and tigers are so closely related that if you shaved them you might not be able to tell them apart. Female lions are the pride's primary hunters. They work together to prey upon large animals that are faster than lions—such as wildebeests and zebras—in the open grasslands. Lions will rest up to 20 hours a day!

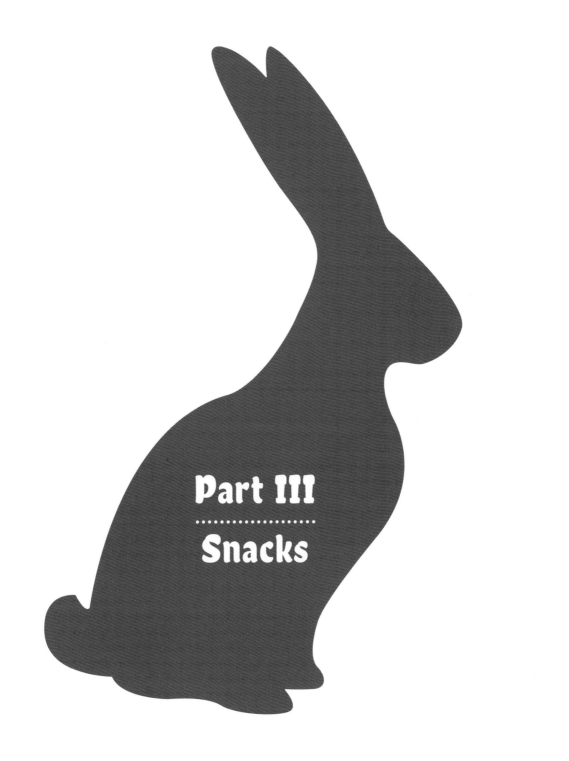

Part III

Snacks

Peachy Parrot

This Peachy Parrot takes just minutes to decorate and is a great way to get your kids to eat a healthy afternoon snack. One peach has ten different vitamins that can be very beneficial to kids. We live in Georgia, the Peach State, and we are always finding interesting and fun ways to use our delicious peaches.

Ingredients

- 2 peaches
- 1 pretzel rod
- 1 marshmallow
- 2 chocolate chips

Directions
• • • • • •

1 Cut one peach in half using a knife and cut out the pit. Place one of the halves on a plate for the body and the other peach half above it for the head.

2 Cut the other peach in half and cut out the pit. Cut one peach half into slices. Place the peach slices on the side of the body to look like wings. Place the pretzel rod under the peach body.

3 Take the other peach half and cut it in half again. Cut the peach quarter into thin slices and place the slices under the pretzel rod to look like feathers on a tail.

4 Using a knife, cut the beak and feet out of the other peach quarter. Cut three small slices from the remaining peach scraps and place them on top of the head to look like feathers. Using kitchen scissors, cut the ends off of a marshmallow and shape them into eyes. Place two chocolate chips on the marshmallow eyes for pupils.

Tips and Tricks

You can use this same idea with any other fruit, but we think that the colors on a peach look the best. You can cut out the eyes from a slice of white cheese in place of the marshmallow. You can also use raisins for the pupils.

Animal Fact

Most parrots live in tropical areas, and there are over 350 different parrot species. Parrots are believed to be one of the most intelligent of all birds, and some of the parrot species are known to imitate human voices. Parrots (especially macaws) can make great pets and are known to have brightly colored feathers. Most parrots eat seeds, fruit, flowers, nuts, and insects for food. Parrots can live to be over eighty years old!

Gorilla Granola Bites

Granola is always a great snack for kids. They will love these fun gorilla cups, and these are very easy to make. My boys love to take these for a school snack or just to have at home for a fun afternoon snack. These can also be served as a special breakfast treat, since there is chocolate involved.

Ingredients

(6-8 servings)

- ¾ cup peanut butter (divided)
- ¼ cup honey
- 2 tablespoons unsweetened cocoa powder
- ¼ teaspoon salt
- 1 ½ cups quick cooking oats
- 1 cup natural cocoa crispy rice cereal
- mini chocolate chips
- marshmallow bits
- chocolate icing
- almonds

Directions
• • • • • •

1 In a medium-sized saucepan over medium heat, add ½ cup peanut butter and honey. Stir until the peanut butter is melted and fully combined with the honey. Add the cocoa powder and salt. Stir until smooth.

2 Remove saucepan from the heat and stir in the oats. When the oats are completely combined, add the cocoa crispy cereal, stirring gently to avoid crushing.

3 Transfer the mixture into 6–8 cups of a muffin pan (depending how full you want them), pressing down firmly and evenly. Cover the muffin pan with foil and place into the fridge to set, about 1 hour.

4 When the mixture has set, remove the chocolate granola cups using a knife. Place the cups on a work surface to decorate the tops.

5 Spread the remaining peanut butter on the tops for the face using a knife. Add two mini chocolate chips for the nose. Cut the marshmallow bits in half for the eyes. Use the chocolate icing to add pupils to the eyes using a toothpick. Squeeze a small amount of icing for the mouth. Attach the almonds on the sides for ears using the icing.

6 Let the icing set for about 10 minutes before serving.

Tips and Tricks

You can use almond or sunflower seed butter to substitute for kids with peanut butter allergies. Make sure to use quick cooking oats for the cups to stick together properly. You can replace the chocolate chips with raisins. You can use dates for the ears, for those with nut allergies.

Animal Fact

Gorillas are very large apes that are native to Africa. There are mountain gorillas and lowland gorillas. Gorillas are herbivores. They like to eat leafy plants, roots, and fruit. Gorillas are known to be very intelligent. Some gorillas have even been taught sign language. Gorillas can live between 30 and 40 years in the wild and up to 50 years at a zoo.

Foxy Fruit Snack

Your kids will love this cute fox on their plate, and this makes a great fall snack. You can also cut out a piece of sliced white cheese to place on top of an orange if your kids prefer that to an apple.

Ingredients

- 1 large light red apple
- 1 pretzel rod
- 2 pretzel sticks
- raisins
- golden raisins
- dried cranberries
- 1 black grape

Directions

1 Cut the red apple in half using a knife. Cut one of the halves in a smaller circle for the fox's head and place it on a plate. Place the other half on the bottom for the body. Save the apple scraps.

2 Using a sharp knife, take the top apple and peel off the sides, leaving a small strip in the middle. Add a little bit of lemon juice on the exposed apple to prevent any browning. Cut out a tail with the apple scraps and also cut the peel off at the tip. Cut out two small ears from the apple scraps and place them on the top sides.

3 Place a pretzel rod on the side of the fox apple. Place two pretzel sticks on the top of the pretzel rod for branches. Take a handful of raisins, golden raisins, and dried cranberries to place under the fox apple. Place more of the raisins and dried cranberries around the branches on the ends.

4 Place a black grape at the bottom of the top apple for the nose. Press on two raisins for the eyes.

Tips and Tricks

You can use a blueberry or chocolate chip for the nose instead of the grape. You can also use any dried fruit combination for the leaves. You can use a red pear in place of the apple.

Animal Fact

Foxes are very social creatures that live in packs. They usually live in the forest, but can also be found in mountains, grasslands, and deserts. Foxes like to hunt at night and like to eat small animals, fruit, vegetables, fish, frogs, and worms. Foxes signal one another by making scent posts such as urinating on trees or rocks to announce their presence. A fox only lives for three to four years in the wild, but can live ten to twelve years in a zoo setting. Foxes have great eyesight and a keen sense of smell; they can run very fast. Overall, they are very intelligent and cunning animals.

Porcupine Pear Pretzel Snack

This is a great after-school snack that gets the kids to eat something healthy and this will put a big smile on their faces. This is also a fun snack for the kids to help create. They will like poking the pretzel sticks into the pear!

Ingredients

- 1 pear
- pretzel sticks
- 1 black grape
- 2 mini chocolate chips

Directions
• • • • • •

1 Wash and cut a pear in half. Cut off the peel just a little ways back from the stem using a knife. Place the half on a plate. Poke holes into the peel part of the pear using a knife. Press pretzel sticks in the holes.

2 Cut off the tip of a black grape. Place the grape tip at the tip of the pear for the nose. Place two chocolate chips above the nose for the eyes.

Tips and Tricks

You can use a raisin in place of the black grape for the nose and eyes. You can use potato sticks in place of the pretzel sticks.

Animal Fact

The porcupine is one of the world's largest and prickliest of rodents. There are over 25 different porcupine species, and they all have a coat of needle-like quills to defend themselves from predators. Porcupines have soft hair mixed in with their sharp quills. These long quills detach easily when touched and can be very painful. Porcupines are herbivores and live between five and seven years in the wild.

Penguin Fruit Snacks

These little penguins are fun to make for parties, especially class parties. These are a huge hit with the kids, and they are very easy to make. You can also replace the fruit with black olives and fill them with cream cheese. However, most kids probably prefer grapes.

Ingredients

- large black grapes
- toothpicks
- ½ (8-ounce) package of cream cheese (softened)
- ½ cup sugar
- ½ 7.5-ounce container Marshmallow Fluff
- 1 cup whipped topping
- ½ teaspoon vanilla
- blue or black sprinkles
- mandarin oranges

Directions

1 Place 2 black grapes on a toothpick and stand them up on a plate. If the grapes are not standing up, you can cut off a thin slice from the bottom to prevent them from rolling.

2 Combine the softened cream cheese, sugar, Marshmallow Fluff, whipped topping, and vanilla in a small bowl. Mix well using an electric mixer. Spoon the fruit dip in a plastic bag and snip off the corner. Squeeze a tiny bit of dip on the top grape for the eyes and add the blue sprinkles for the pupils. Squeeze more dip on the front of the bottom grape for the belly. Smooth out the dip with a knife.

3 Cut the mandarin orange slices in half and place two on the bottom for feet. Cut the tips off the mandarin orange slices and press the tips on the face under the eyes for the beak. Cut thin slices from the grapes to make wings. You can attach the wings and orange beak with a little bit of the dip using a toothpick.

Tips and Tricks

You can cut mini marshmallows in half and press them on the fronts of the grapes for the belly in place of the fruit dip. You can use cheddar cheese or carrots instead of the oranges for the feet and beak.

Animal Fact

Penguins are known to huddle together to escape wind and keep warm. Individual penguins take turns moving to the inside of the huddle. Once the penguin is warm it will move to the outside of the group so that others can have protection. Female penguins lay a single egg and then promptly leave it behind. The males will keep the newly laid eggs warm, but they do not sit on them. They balance the eggs on their feet and cover them with their feathered skin. They do this for about two months with nothing to eat. When the female penguins return they bring a belly full of food that they regurgitate for the baby penguins to eat.

Apple Owl

This Apple Owl is a great way to get the kids to eat a healthy afternoon snack after school. This fun owl is so easy to make, you can create it in less than ten minutes. Apples of any color will work for this fun idea.

Ingredients

- 2 apples
- 1 black grape
- 1 pretzel rod
- 2 mandarin orange slices
- 3 green grapes

Directions

• • • • • •

1 Cut one of the apples in half. Place the apple halves on a plate using one for the body and one for the head. Cut the other apple in half and cut one of the halves into slices. Place the slices on the sides of the apple body to look like wings.

2 Cut out two tufts from the apple scraps and place them on the top apple. Cut a thick slice from the other apple half and cut two small circles from that slice. Place the apple circles on the top apple to look like eyes. Cut a black grape in half for the pupils.

3 Place a pretzel rod below the bottom apple. Take your two mandarin orange slices and cut them in half. Place the mandarin orange halved slices on the bottom for the feet and another slice on the top apple for the beak.

4 Cut green grapes in half and add them on the end of the pretzel rod to look like leaves.

Tips and Tricks

You can also use other fruits in place of the apple to make this creation, including a pear, peach, etc. You can replace the apple eyes with marshmallows and replace the grape (the pupils) using raisins. You can replace the green grapes using kiwi or lettuce. You can replace the orange slices with cheddar cheese.

Animal Fact

There are around 200 different owl species in the world. Owls are nocturnal and very active at night. Owls have large eyes, which enhances their night vision. Most owls hunt insects, small mammals, and other birds. Owls are powerful birds and fiercely protective parents. Owls are known to make a *hooo-hooo* sound. The colors on an owl's feathers help them to blend in with the environment.

Froggy Fruit Snack

My boys have always been picky fruit eaters and would never even think of trying a kiwi. That was until this fun frog snack came along. They not only tried the kiwi; they loved the kiwi! If you do not have a blue plate, you can always add a handful of blueberries around the frogs to look like water.

Ingredients

- 1 apple
- 2 kiwis
- 4 green grapes
- 5 raisins
- 1 strawberry
- toothpicks

Directions
• • • • • •

1 Cut three slices from the apple and also cut out a small wedge from each side using a knife. Place two apple slices on a plate to look like lily pads. Peel the kiwis and cut them in half. Place two halves down on the apple slices (one half atop each slice) with the flat sides down. Place the other kiwi halves, with the flat sides up, atop the first kiwi halves, securing with a toothpick.

2 Cut two eyes from the remaining apple slice and place them on top of the kiwi. Use toothpick halves to secure if needed. Cut the green grapes in half and place them on the sides of the kiwi to look like legs and feet.

3 Cut raisins in half and press the raisin halves using the cut sides on the apple eyes to make pupils. Slice a strawberry and then cut off a strip for the tongue and mouth. Press them on the front of the kiwi. Cut off pieces of a raisin for the nose and place a raisin on the bottom of the strawberry tongue to look like a fly. You can use pieces of apple scraps to make little wings on the fly.

Tips and Tricks

You can add a little bit of lemon juice to the apple to prevent browning while you decorate your fruit snack. You can replace the raisins with chocolate chips. A sliced pear or pineapple can replace the apple.

Animal Fact

There are over 4,000 different species of frogs around the world. Frogs can see forward, upward, and sideways at the same time. They even sleep with their eyes open. A frog is an amphibian. They lay their eggs under water, and the eggs hatch into tadpoles. The tadpole lives in the water until it turns into an adult frog. Frogs can live both on land and in the water. Frogs use their sticky tongue to catch and swallow food. Small frogs like to eat insects, such as flies, mosquitoes, and dragonflies. Larger frogs like to eat worms and grasshoppers.

Sheep Snack

Banana slices give a nice fluffy fleece look to this fun sheep snack. This makes a nice snack for springtime or Easter. This is also a great way to get the kids to eat a healthy after-school snack!

Ingredients

- 1 banana
- 5 black grapes
- 2 mini marshmallows
- 1 raisin
- green grapes

Directions
• • • • • •

1   Using a knife, peel and cut the banana into slices. Place the banana slices on a plate, leaving a hole in the middle. Cut the black grapes in half and place 8 halves in the middle of the sliced bananas for the head. Place two grape halves on the bottom for the feet.

2   Cut the mini marshmallows in half. Place two marshmallow halves on the head for eyes. Cut off pieces from the other marshmallow half for the nose. Cut the raisin in half using kitchen scissors and place them on the marshmallow halves for pupils.

3   Using a knife, cut a handful of green grapes in half. Place the grape halves on the bottom of the plate, lining them up to look like grass.

Tips and Tricks

You can use blueberries or blackberries in place of the black grapes. You can use lettuce or sliced kiwi for the grass instead of the green grapes.

Animal Fact

Sheep are very intelligent animals and are actually capable of problem solving. They are almost as clever as pigs. Sheep are known to self-medicate when they get sick. They will eat specific plants to help cure themselves. Female sheep are very caring mothers that create a deep bond with their lambs. The mothers can recognize their lambs by their call if they wander too far away.

Part IV
·············
Dinner

Chili Cat

Your little kitty cat lovers will adore this chili! This fun chili is also a great way to hide lots of veggies and they will never even notice. Quinoa is one of the most protein-rich foods around and contains almost twice as much fiber as most of the other grains. My picky eaters love this chili recipe, especially how it's decorated.

Ingredients

(4 servings)

- 1 cup uncooked quinoa, rinsed
- 2 cups water
- 1 tablespoon vegetable oil
- 1 onion, chopped
- 4 cloves garlic, chopped
- ½ tablespoon chili powder
- 1 tablespoon ground cumin
- 1 (28-ounce) can crushed tomatoes
- 2 (19-ounce) cans black beans, rinsed and drained
- ½ green bell pepper, chopped
- 1 red bell pepper, chopped
- 1 zucchini, chopped
- 1 slice of cheddar cheese
- sour cream
- potato sticks

Directions
• • • • • •

1 Bring the quinoa and water to a boil in a saucepan over high heat. Reduce heat to medium-low, cover, and simmer until the quinoa is tender, and the water has been absorbed, about 15 to 20 minutes; set aside.

2 Meanwhile, heat the vegetable oil in a large pot over medium heat. Stir in the chopped onion, and cook until the onion softens and turns translucent, about five minutes. Add the garlic, chili powder, and cumin; cook and stir one minute. Stir in the tomatoes, black beans (reserving some for the eyes), green bell pepper, red bell pepper, and zucchini. Season with salt and pepper to taste. Bring to a simmer over high heat, then reduce heat to medium-low; cover and let simmer for 20 minutes.

3 Stir in the reserved quinoa after the 20 minutes. Cut out the ears and nose from the slice of cheddar cheese using a knife. Spoon a little bit of sour cream in a plastic bag and snip off the corner. Pipe the mouth and eyes on with the sour cream. Place the reserved black beans on the eyes for pupils. Press in three potato sticks on each side to look like whiskers.

Tips and Tricks

You can cut out the mouth and eyes from a slice of white cheese, such as provolone or Swiss, in place of the sour cream. You can use pretzel sticks in place of the potato sticks. Any kind of chili recipe would work well for this fun idea.

Animal Fact

Cats are one of the most popular pets in the world! There are over 500 million domestic or stray cats worldwide. Cats have very flexible bodies and are very sneaky for hunting small animals like mice and rats. Cats have very powerful night vision, excellent hearing, and a strong sense of smell. Cats spend about fourteen to sixteen hours a day sleeping and spend most of their waking hours cleaning themselves. An average cat lives to be twelve to fifteen years old.

"Hippo"tato Soup

Soup is a very hard thing to get your picky eaters to try, especially when any veggies are involved. My boys insist that this is the most fantastic soup recipe on earth and have never even noticed the carrots and onion included. They also have fun pretend-playing with their "Hippo"tato swimming in his soup.

Ingredients

- ½ large onion, chopped
- 1 clove garlic, chopped
- 3 tablespoons butter
- 1 bag (15–17 per bag) of multicolored small potatoes (peeled and diced, saving 2 purple potatoes to decorate)
- 5 baby carrots, diced
- 3 cups water
- 2 large chicken bouillon cubes
- ground black pepper to taste
- 3 tablespoons all-purpose flour
- 3 cups milk
- ½ tablespoon dried parsley
- ½ teaspoon dried thyme
- sour cream
- raisins

Directions

1 Melt the butter in a saucepan over medium heat. Stir in the chopped onion and garlic; cook and stir until the onion has softened and turned translucent, about five to eight minutes.

2 While the onions are cooking, place the diced potatoes, carrots, water, and chicken bouillon in another pot and bring to a boil. Cook until carrots and potatoes are tender, about 10 minutes or so. Try not to overcook. Season with black pepper to taste.

3 Add the flour to the cooked onions to make a paste. Cook, stirring constantly, for about three minutes. Gradually add the milk and stir well. Cook over low heat, stirring constantly, until warmed through. Add the potato and carrot mixture. Stir in the parsley and thyme and heat through.

4 Cook the two reserved purple potatoes in the microwave until cooked through. Cut a small slit on the side of one of the potatoes to make a mouth. Spoon the soup into a bowl. Place the potatoes in the soup. Add a little bit of sour cream on the end of a toothpick to "paint" on the teeth. Add a little more sour cream for the eyes using your toothpick. Place on two raisins for the ears and cut two small pieces from another raisin to use for the pupils.

Tips and Tricks

Make sure to dice up your veggies very well. Big chunks of veggies might not be appealing to picky eaters. You can also make a hippo out of a dark brown roll to place in the soup instead of using purple potatoes.

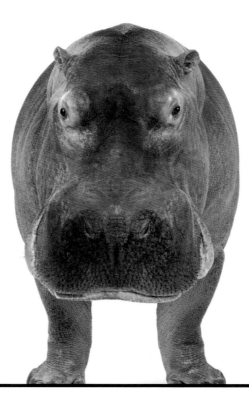

Animal Fact

The name *hippopotamus* means "river horse," because they love to spend most of their day hanging out in the water. They are native to Africa, and the water helps them to keep cool in the hot African sun. Hippos are great swimmers and can hold their breath underwater for up to five minutes! At sunset the hippos leave the water and travel on land to graze. A hippo can eat up to 80 pounds of grass each night. Hippos are very fast for their size and can also be very dangerous. A hippo can live up to 40 years in the wild.

Mini Shepherd's Sheep Pies

You can easily turn this family favorite dinner into these cute little sheep. This is also a great springtime or Easter meal that the kids will just love!

Ingredients

- 1 package of large homestyle biscuits
- ½ tablespoon olive oil
- ½ onion (chopped)
- 16 ounces ground turkey
- ½ teaspoon minced garlic
- ½ cup shredded cheddar cheese
- premade mashed potatoes (cooked)
- 1 black olive

Directions

• • • • • •

1 Heat the oven to 350 degrees F. Spray a muffin pan with cooking spray. Open the package of biscuits and press each biscuit into the muffin pan, on the bottoms and up the sides.

2 Add the olive oil to a pan on medium heat. Add the chopped onion and sauté until translucent for about four minutes. Add the ground turkey and garlic and cook until there is no pink showing. Drain after cooking.

3 Sprinkle a pinch of the shredded cheddar cheese on the bottom of the biscuits. Then add the ground turkey mixture, leaving just a little bit of room on the top. Keep aside some of the ground turkey for decorating.

4 Add the cooked mashed potatoes to a frosting decorator or scoop the potatoes in a plastic bag and snip off the corner. Pipe the mashed potatoes on top of the filled biscuits, making large dots.

5 Press in the reserved ground turkey mixture, making the head, ears, and little feet. Pipe just a little more of the mashed potatoes on top of the ground turkey head.

6 Bake at 375 degrees F for about 20 to 25 minutes. When they are done baking, add a little bit of the mashed potatoes on the head for eyes using a toothpick. Chop up tiny pieces from the black olive and place them on the face to make pupils and a nose.

Tips and Tricks

You can replace the ground turkey with beef. You can use any kind of cheese or just eliminate the cheese. You can replace the black olive with a raisin.

Animal Fact

China has more sheep than any other country, and there are over 1 billion sheep in the entire world! Female adult sheep are known as ewes and male sheep are known as rams. Young sheep are known as lambs. Sheep are herbivores and love to eat grass. France uses the milk of sheep to make Roquefort cheese and Greece uses the milk of sheep to make feta cheese. The wool of sheep is used for the fiber from the fleece, which is durable, wrinkle-resistant, fire-resistant, and insulating. The fabric is used to make sweaters, blankets, coats, and much more!

Penguin Black Bean Soup

This black bean soup is a great way to sneak in lots of veggies in the kids' dinner. I have made this black bean soup for years and this is a favorite of my boys. You can decorate this little penguin in just minutes. This fun idea can also be used for chili as well!

Ingredients

- 1 tablespoon olive oil
- 1 onion, finely chopped
- 1 teaspoon minced garlic
- 4 baby carrots, chopped
- 1 teaspoon chili powder
- 1 tablespoon cumin
- pinch black pepper
- 4 cups vegetable broth
- 4 (15-ounce) cans black beans (reserving a few beans for decorating)
- 1 (15-ounce) can whole kernel corn
- 1 (14.5-ounce) can crushed tomatoes
- ¼ cup sour cream
- 1 slice dark German wheat bread
- 1 baby carrot

Directions

· · · · · ·

1 Heat the olive oil in a large pot over medium-high heat. Sauté the chopped onion, garlic, and carrots for four minutes. Season with chili powder, cumin, and black pepper, cooking for two minutes. Stir in vegetable broth, two cans of black beans, and corn. Bring the mixture to a boil.

2 Meanwhile, in a blender, process the remaining two cans of black beans and tomatoes until smooth. Stir the bean mixture into the boiling soup. Reduce the heat to medium and simmer for about 15 minutes. Spoon the black bean soup into bowls.

3 Spoon the sour cream in a plastic bag and snip off the corner. Squeeze the sour cream on top of the soup to look like the belly of a penguin. You can use a knife to spread the sour cream evenly. Do the same for the eyes. Place on two black beans for the pupils.

4 Toast the slice of dark German wheat bread and cut the slice in half. Place the halves on the sides of the soup to look like flippers. Cut the other baby carrot in half using a knife. Cut out the feet and beak from the carrot halves and place them on top of the soup.

Tips and Tricks

You can replace the sour cream with a slice of provolone cheese. You can chop up any veggies your kids like to hide in this soup, including celery, zucchini, etc. Just make sure to chop up the veggies finely. You can add extra chili powder if your kids do not mind spicy foods.

Animal Fact

Penguins can be found on every continent in the Southern Hemisphere. Penguins cannot fly like other birds. Instead of wings they have adapted flippers to help them swim in the water. Penguins eat several different kinds of fish and other sea life that they find underwater. Emperor penguins are the largest of all penguins, standing on average 45 inches tall. Little blue penguins are the smallest type of penguin, with an average height of 13 inches.

Dinodilla Dinner

You will be a hero with most kids, especially little boys, when you make this dinosaur quesadilla for their dinner. This is also a great way to get the kids to eat lots of black beans, a spinach tortilla, and brown rice.

Ingredients

- 2 spinach tortillas
- ½ cup black beans
- ½ cup shredded cheddar cheese
- ¼ cup of brown rice (cooked)
- sour cream

Directions

• • • • • •

1 Cut the two spinach tortillas in half using kitchen scissors. Shape one of the halves of each tortilla into a circle. Cut out triangle shapes around the curved edge of the other half of each tortilla, leaving a small curve in the middle along the flat side for the mouth. Save the scraps for later use.

2 Sprinkle half of the black beans (reserving five for decorating), cheese, and brown rice on one of the circular tortilla halves. Top with the other circular tortilla half. Repeat this with the same jagged-edged tortilla halves.

3 You can either fry the quesadillas in a pan or place them in the microwave for one minute until the cheese is completely melted. Place the cooked quesadillas on a plate, with the round quesadilla toward the bottom of the plate and the pointed quesadilla at the top. Cut out the feet and a tail with the tortilla scraps. Place the feet on the bottom and the tail on the side of the body.

4 Spoon on a little bit of sour cream on the head for the eyes and a small amount for the horn. Cut the reserved black beans in half and place them on the feet, nose, and eyes.

Tips and Tricks

You can use any fillings for the quesadilla, including veggies. When you cut out one tortilla use that as a guide to cut out the other one instead of cutting them together. You can also use a regular flour tortilla if you do not have a spinach tortilla, and spread guacamole on top to make the dinosaur green.

Animal Fact

Dinosaurs ruled the earth for over 160 million years. The Tyrannosaurus rex was one of the largest meat-eating dinosaurs that ever lived. It measured up to 40 feet long and about 15 to 20 feet tall! The smallest dinosaur was the Compsognathus ("pretty jaw"), which measured three feet long . . . about the size of a chicken. A person that studies dinosaurs is called a paleontologist. It's believed that dinosaurs lived on earth until around 65 million years ago, when they became extinct.

Mexican Stuffed Froggy Peppers

These Mexican stuffed peppers contain healthy ingredients that the kids will love. I never thought my boys would try a stuffed pepper, but how could any kid resist eating these adorable frogs?! Now this is one of their most requested dinners.

Ingredients

- 1 cup uncooked quinoa, rinsed
- 5 green bell peppers, seeds removed
- 1 (15-ounce) can black beans, drained and rinsed
- 1 (14.5-ounce) can diced tomatoes and green chilies
- ¼ teaspoon salt
- ¼ teaspoon pepper
- 1 can mild enchilada sauce
- 1 cup cheddar cheese (divided in half)
- 1 Roma tomato
- sour cream

Directions

1 Add the quinoa to a large saucepan with two cups of water and a pinch of salt. Bring to a boil over medium-high heat. Boil five minutes, cover, turn off the heat, and let it steam for 15 minutes. Fluff with a fork.

2 Cut the tops off the green bell peppers and save them for decorating. Scoop out the seeds using a spoon. Microwave the peppers on a plate for two to three minutes to soften slightly. (You can also skip this step if you like a crispier pepper).

3 Pour the quinoa into a mixing bowl. Stir in the black beans (saving about 10 of them to decorate), tomato with green chilies and their juices, ¼ tsp salt, ¼ tsp pepper, enchilada sauce, and ½ cup of cheese.

4 Place the peppers in a 9x13-inch baking dish. Divide filling among peppers. Sprinkle the remaining cheese on top.

5 Cover the peppers with foil and bake at 375 degrees F for 25 to 30 minutes. Remove the foil and cook about five minutes longer. Once the peppers are done cooking you can start decorating them into frogs.

6 Using a knife, cut pieces from the reserved tops of the peppers to make the back legs, front legs, and feet. Place them at the sides of the peppers. Cut off strips of the Roma tomato for the tongues and press them on the front using the flesh side to stick. Use a spoon to place the sour cream on top for the eyes. Take the reserved black beans and add one to each scoop of sour cream for the pupil. Add another black bean on the bottoms of the tongue to look like a fly. You can add a tiny amount of sour cream on the sides of the black beans using a toothpick to look like little wings.

Tips and Tricks

You can use also use pieces of a red bell or roasted pepper in place of the tomato to make the tongue. You can replace the quinoa with brown rice. If your kids do not like sour cream you can cut a mini round cheese snack in half to make the eyes.

Animal Fact

Frogs are amphibians and are cold-blooded, which means that their bodies are the same temperature as the water or air around them. They can be found around bodies of fresh, slow-moving water including ponds, lakes, and marshes. They can also be found on land and in trees. Frogs have long legs that are great for hopping, skin that is smooth, and pads on their toes that make them great at climbing.

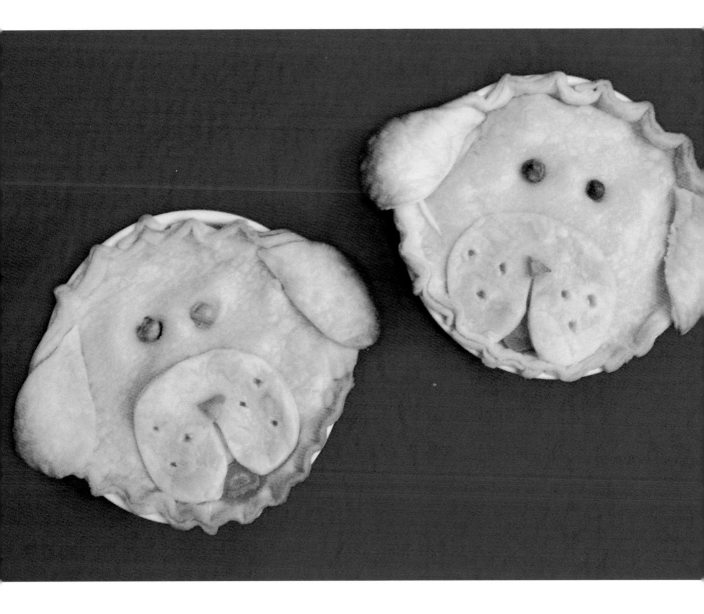

Puppy Pot Pies

Chicken pot pie is a great way to get your kids to eat lots of veggies. Most kids love pot pie, but my boys would never even try it (it's a texture thing). These cute puppy pot pies got my boys to try potpie for the first time, and they loved it!

Ingredients

(serves 4)

- 1 sliced carrot
- 1 cup chopped carrots
- ½ cup frozen green peas
- 1-pound bag of frozen cubed chicken, thawed
- 2 (9-inch) unbaked pie crusts
- ¼ cup chopped onion

- ⅓ cup butter
- ⅓ cup all-purpose flour
- ½ teaspoon salt
- ¼ teaspoon black pepper
- ¼ teaspoon celery seed
- 1 can of chicken broth
- ⅔ cup milk

Directions
• • • • • •

1 Preheat oven to 425 degrees F.

2 Cut eight slices from carrot. Chop up the rest of your carrots very well. Put your chopped carrots and peas (including eight carrot slices) with the diced chicken in a large pot. Cover the ingredients with water. Bring to a boil for 15 minutes. Remove from heat and set aside. Also set aside your eight cooked carrot slices and eight of the cooked peas to decorate your puppy face.

3 Roll out your pie crust. We used 4 (6-ounce) soufflé dishes. Place a soufflé dish on the crust and cut a circle an inch or so beyond the dish. Place the bottom crust in the dish. Press down the bottom and sides. There should be some of the crust sticking out around the top. Make sure to save any of the pie dough scraps to decorate the face and for the ears.

4 In a saucepan over medium heat, cook the onion in the butter until soft. Stir in the flour, salt, pepper, and celery seed. Slowly stir in chicken broth and milk. Simmer over medium-low heat until thick, about five to eight minutes. When thickened up, you can remove from heat.

5 Place the chicken mixture in the bottom of the pie crusts and pour the flour/milk mixture over the top. Cover with the top crust, seal edges, and cut away excess dough. Press down on the sides a bit to prevent any of the mixture from coming out. We pinched ours to make it look like puppy hair. We made two small holes in the top where the eyes go and the nose to allow steam to escape.

6 Roll out the dough scraps and cut out four smaller circles for the nose. Cut out one ear and use that as a guide to cut out the rest. Poke a few holes on each side of the nose. Cut out and cut a slit down the middle. Place the saved carrots on for the nose and tongue. Put the peas on for the eyes and place the nose cutout on the face. Press on the ears. Some will hang off the sides.

7 Bake in your preheated oven for 25 to 30 minutes, or until pastry is golden brown and filling is bubbly. Cover your pies with foil about halfway through the baking if they are browning quickly.

Tips and Tricks

You can use any chicken pot pie recipe to make this. Just make sure to split it up into four small dishes. You can add in any veggies that your kids like, or take out any veggies that they don't like. You can make one large pot pie in place of the four individual dishes. Just make the eyes and mouth larger using your veggies.

Animal Fact

The size of a puppy depends on the breed of the dog. When puppies are born they are blind, deaf, and toothless. Puppies depend on their mother and siblings to cuddle up for warmth. Puppies sleep a lot and spend up to 18 to 19 hours sleeping in a 24-hour day. Puppies need to eat smaller meals 3 to 4 times a day to help them digest their food.

Mexican Billy Goat Quesadilla

We love to eat Mexican food in our house, and we are always coming up with fun ways to make quesadillas. This is a great way to load the kids up on black beans and brown rice. You can also add lots of your kid's favorite sautéed veggies inside the quesadilla to make this a healthier dinner.

Ingredients

- 2 large flour tortillas
- black beans
- brown rice (cooked)
- shredded cheese
- shredded lettuce
- sour cream
- 1 small yellow bell pepper

Directions

● ● ● ● ● ●

1 Cut out two circles from a large flour tortilla, making one just a bit larger than the other one, using kitchen scissors. Use those pieces as a guide to cut the other tortilla. Save the scraps for decorating.

2 Place two of the tortillas (one large circle and one smaller one) on a work surface. Top the tortillas with the black beans, brown rice, and shredded cheese. Place the other cutout tortillas on top. Grill or microwave for one minute until the cheese is completely melted.

3 Place your prepared quesadillas on a plate, using the larger quesadilla for the body and the smaller quesadilla for the head. Place shredded lettuce on the bottom to look like grass.

4 Spoon some sour cream in a plastic bag. Snip off the corner and pipe on the horns, eyes, and beard. Place two black beans on the eyes for pupils and two black beans for the nose.

5 Cut four black beans in half using a knife for the collar and feet. Cut one black bean into thin strips to make the mouth. Cut off a piece of the yellow bell pepper into a triangle shape and place it on the collar to look like a little bell. Take your tortilla scraps and cut out ears and a tail.

Tips and Tricks

You can use slices of white cheese if your kids do not like the sour cream. You can use avocado for the grass. Use any filling for the quesadilla— this is a great way to slip in some hidden veggies.

Animal Fact

Goats were among one of the first domesticated animals. Goats can have short or long hair along with curled, silky, or coarse hair. They have wattles on their necks and beards. Goats come in different colors including solid black, red, white, or brown, and they can be spotted or have blended shades. Goats like to eat shrubs, trees, hay, weeds, and grain, but are also known to eat just about anything. A goat's pupils give it excellent side-to-side vision without having to move its head.

Part V

Treats

Mini Moose Mousse Cups

This simple and fun dessert can be created by the kids all by themselves. This mousse recipe is creamy and delicious. Your kids will not only love the way these look, but they will also fall in love with how they taste!

Ingredients

(4 servings)
- 1 ½ cups milk, divided
- ¼ cup semisweet chocolate chips
- 1 package (1.4-ounce) chocolate instant pudding
- 1 ½ cups whipped topping
- Tootsie Rolls
- pretzel twists
- mini marshmallows
- mini chocolate chips
- chocolate chips

Directions
● ● ● ● ● ●

1 Microwave one cup of milk and ¼ cup chocolate chips in a large microwavable bowl on high for two minutes. Whisk until the chocolate is melted. Add the remaining milk and dry chocolate pudding mix. Beat with an electric mixer for two to three minutes. Refrigerate 15 minutes. Whisk in 1 ½ cups whipped topping. Spoon the mixture into dessert dishes.

2 Place a Tootsie Roll in the microwave for seven to eight seconds until lightly softened. Cut the Tootsie Roll in half and shape the halves into ears. Place the Tootsie Roll ears in the sides of the chocolate mousse cups. Break the pretzel twists to resemble antlers and place them on the top sides above the ears. Cut the mini marshmallows in half and place them on the top for eyes. Place mini chocolate chips on top of the marshmallow halves for pupils. Place on two chocolate chips for the nose.

Tips and Tricks

You can also make this dessert using chocolate ice cream, cookies, or cupcakes. If you do not have marshmallows, you can use candy eyes. You can break off pieces from a premade chocolate cookie to make the ears.

Animal Fact

Moose are the largest of all of the deer family and have huge antlers that can measure over six feet wide. The male moose (which is called a bull) sheds his antlers every spring and grows new antlers in the winter. They can weigh up to 1,500 pounds and measure up to six feet tall. A moose can run pretty fast—up to 35 miles per hour! Moose love to eat plants and also love to spend time in the water. They are known to be great swimmers. The average life span of a moose is between 15 and 20 years.

Beaver Brownie Bites

These itty bitty Beaver Brownie Bites are so adorable and can be created in just minutes. This sweet snack is fun to make for the kids at home, or would be really cute to make for preschool classes learning the letter B. You can also purchase premade brownie bites from the grocery store to make these even easier!

Ingredients

(48 brownie bites)
- ¾ cup butter, softened
- 1 cup sugar
- ¼ cup brown sugar
- 1 tablespoon water
- 1 ½ teaspoons vanilla extract
- 2 eggs
- 1 ½ cups all-purpose flour
- ½ cup cocoa
- ¼ teaspoon salt
- ¼ teaspoon baking soda
- chocolate chips
- chocolate cookie icing
- mini chocolate chips
- marshmallow bits
- black edible marker
- pretzel spoons

Directions
• • • • • •

1 Beat the softened butter, granulated sugar, brown sugar, water, and vanilla in a large bowl with a mixer on medium speed until completed blended. Add the eggs and beat well. In a separate bowl, stir together the flour, cocoa, salt, and baking soda. Gradually add the dry ingredients to the sugar mixture, beating on low speed until blended. Cover and refrigerate dough about one to two hours or until slightly firm.

2 Preheat the oven to 350 degrees F. Spray mini muffin tins with cooking spray. Shape the dough into one-inch balls and place the balls into the prepared mini muffin cups.

3 Bake for 12 minutes or until the top looks set. Make sure to not overbake. Cool completely before decorating.

4 Attach two chocolate chips on the top sides using the chocolate icing. Make a mouth with the chocolate icing. Place on the mini chocolate chip for the nose. Cut a marshmallow in half and place on the bottom of the mouth to look like teeth. Cut a marshmallow bit in half and attach on the front for the eyes. Press a black edible marker in the middle to make a dot for the pupil.

5 Break the pretzel spoons in half. Cut a small slit in the back of the brownie bite using a knife. Squeeze a little bit of the chocolate icing on the broken side of the pretzel spoon half. Press the pretzel into the slit on the back of the brownie bite.

Tips and Tricks

You can use any boxed brownie mix in place of this recipe. You can use any small rounded cookie for the tail in place of the pretzel spoon. You can also use regular muffin-size cups, replace the marshmallow bits with mini marshmallows (cut in half), and substitute the regular-sized chocolate chips with large chocolate chips for the ears.

Animal Fact

Beavers are the largest of the rodents and are known to keep very busy. Beavers love to swim and can do so at speeds up to five miles an hour! They can keep themselves underwater for 15 minutes without surfacing and have transparent eyelids that resemble goggles. Their fur is waterproof. Beavers prefer to eat leaves, roots, plants, twigs, and bark. Beavers use their strong teeth and powerful jaws to create massive structures out of logs, branches, and mud, known as dams, to block streams. A beaver can live up to 24 years.

Turtle Turtle Cake

We originally created this cute cake for my husband's birthday a while back. He loves the combo of DeMet's Turtle flavors, including caramel, pecan, and chocolate. My boys wanted to make him some sort of an animal cake. We thought that it was fitting to turn his Turtle cake into a cake that actually looked like a turtle! This is very easy to make and one of my personal all-time favorite cake recipes!

Ingredients

- German chocolate cake mix
- 1 bag of caramels
- ⅓ cup milk
- 8 tablespoons butter
- 6 ounces chocolate chips
- 1 cup of chopped pecans
- chocolate frosting
- pecan halves
- 2 large edible eyes
- 1 red licorice string

Directions
• • • • • •

1 Preheat the oven to 350 degrees F.

2 Make the cake mix according to the package directions. Spray a nonstick 8-inch round cake pan, muffin pan, and soufflé dish with cooking spray. Using only half the batter, fill each of your pans only slightly less than halfway full, filling only four cups of your muffin pan. Place in the oven for 15 to 20 minutes.

3 While that is baking, melt the caramels, milk, and butter in a saucepan on low heat until completely melted. Take the cakes out of the oven and pour the caramel mixture over each cake. Sprinkle with the chocolate chips and the chopped nuts. Pour the remaining cake batter on top and put them back in the oven for 20 minutes at 250 degrees F. Then bring the temperature back up to 350 degrees F for 5 to 10 minutes. Cool the cakes and then remove them from the pans to start decorating.

4 Place the 8-inch cake on a platter and frost the tops and sides with the chocolate frosting. Place the cupcakes on the sides to look like legs and frost. Place the soufflé dish cake on the top for the head and add frosting.

5 Add the pecan halves on the top of the cake to look like a turtle shell. Place two large edible eyes on the top of the head and the licorice string on the front for the mouth.

Tips and Tricks

Chop up the pecans for the cake filling very fine. Lots of kids do not like the texture of large nut pieces in cakes or breads. You can replace the large edible eyes with marshmallows and chocolate chips.

Animal Fact

Turtles are reptiles with a hard shell that protects them like a shield. Leatherbacks are the largest turtles on earth. Some turtles can grow up to seven feet long and get to over 2,000 pounds!

Like other reptiles, turtles are cold-blooded. Some turtles lay eggs in the sand and leave them to hatch all on their own. The baby turtles make their way to the top of the sand and scramble to the water trying to avoid predators. Some of them do not make it. Sea turtles have special glands that help them to remove the salt from the water that they drink.

Koala Pretzel Tree Pops

This is a fun pop that is completely edible! Koalas are so cute and look so lovable. This treat is very easy to create and would be so cute for a jungle- or animal-themed party.

Ingredients

- pretzel rods
- coconut marshmallows
- green chocolate leaves
- chocolate-covered sunflower seeds
- black sprinkles
- 1 bag of butterscotch or peanut butter chips

Directions

• • • • • •

1 Place your pretzel rods, coconut marshmallows, chocolate leaves, sunflower seeds, and sprinkles on a work surface. Place the butterscotch or peanut butter chips in a bowl, reserving some of the chips for the ears. Melt the chips in the microwave for 30 seconds. Stir the chips and repeat heating every 20 seconds, stirring in between, until completed melted. Make sure you do not overheat.

2 Attach two coconut marshmallows on the side of the pretzel rod using the melted butterscotch. Dip two of the chips in the melted butterscotch and add them to the sides of the top marshmallows to look like ears. Use a toothpick and add the melted butterscotch to the front of the top marshmallow for the eyes and nose. Place on the black sprinkles for the eyes and the chocolate-covered sunflower seed for the nose.

3 Add a little of the melted butterscotch to the backside tips of the chocolate leaves using a toothpick. Press the leaves on the top of the pretzel rod.

4 Take the rest of the melted butterscotch and spoon it in a plastic bag. Snip off the corner. Pipe the arms and legs onto wax paper. Let that set and then attach the arms and legs on top of the bottom marshmallow to look like they are grabbing the tree.

Tips and Tricks

You will have to work quickly with the melted butterscotch before it hardens. If it does harden, just place the bowl back in the microwave for 20 seconds until it melts again. You can find the green chocolate leaves at any crafts store. If you cannot find the leaves, you can buy green candy melts and pipe the melts onto wax paper, shaping them into leaves.

Animal Fact

Koalas are native to Australia. They have big round ears and oval noses. Like kangaroos, koalas have pouches in which they carry their newborns. Koalas are herbivores and only eat eucalyptus leaves, mostly at night. They sleep up to 18 hours a day! Koalas have sharp claws that help them climb trees. Koalas also have fingerprints very similar to those of humans.

Beary Cute Cupcakes

We originally created this fun idea to celebrate my son's birthday during our camping trip. These bear cupcakes are a cute idea for a camping excursion or an animal-themed party. They are very easy to make, topped with premade wafer cookies and candies.

Ingredients

- 1 ½ cups granulated sugar
- 1 cup all-purpose flour
- ½ cup cake flour
- 1 cup unsweetened cocoa powder
- 1½ teaspoons baking powder
- 1 teaspoon baking soda
- ½ teaspoon salt
- 1 cup (2 sticks) cold unsalted butter, cut into small cubes
- 4 eggs
- 1 cup sour cream
- 2 teaspoons vanilla extract
- No. 233 multi-opening icing tip
- vanilla wafers
- mini vanilla wafers
- black pearl sprinkles
- chocolate M&Ms
- premade chocolate cookie icing
- toothpicks

Chocolate Buttercream Frosting
- 2 cups of unsalted butter, at room temperature
- 5 cups powdered sugar
- 2 teaspoons vanilla extract
- 8 ounces semisweet chocolate chips, melted and cooled
- 1 tablespoon milk

Cupcake Directions

* * * * * * * * * * * *

1   Preheat the oven to 350 degrees F and line a large muffin pan with 12 large cupcake liners.

2   Place the sugar, flour, cake flour, cocoa, baking powder, baking soda, and salt in a large mixing bowl, and stir to combine all the ingredients.

3   Mix in the butter on low speed, until the mixture resembles moist crumbs.

4   Stir in the eggs, sour cream, and vanilla, scraping the bottom and sides of the bowl to be sure all the ingredients are well incorporated.

5   Fill the cupcake liners just a little over halfway full.

6   Bake for 20 to 25 minutes, or until a cake tester inserted in the center of a cupcake comes out clean or with moist crumbs.

7   Cool completely before frosting and decorating.

8   Once the cake is cooled, scoop the frosting (see below for recipe) in a cake decorating bag using a no. 233 multi-opening tip. Pipe the chocolate frosting on top of the cupcakes to look like hair. Place your mini vanilla wafers on a work surface and attach toothpicks on the back side using the chocolate cookie icing. Let that set for about 10 minutes. Place the mini wafers on the top sides to look like ears. Pipe frosting around the edges, leaving only the middle of the wafer showing.

9   Add a regular vanilla wafer on the front and using icing, attach a chocolate M&M on top to look like a nose. Place black pearl sprinkles above the nose for the eyes.

Frosting Directions

. . . .

1 Using the wire whisk attachment of your stand mixer, whip the butter on medium-high speed for five minutes, stopping to scrape the bowl once or twice.

2 Reduce the speed to low and gradually add in the powdered sugar. Once all of the powdered sugar is incorporated, increase the speed to medium-high and add the vanilla, mixing until incorporated. Melt the chocolate on the stovetop over low heat or in the microwave. For the microwave you can heat the chocolate chips in a bowl for one minute on medium high. Stir, then check every 20 seconds (stirring every time), making sure you do not burn the chocolate. Add the melted chocolate and milk to the powdered-sugar mixture and whip at medium-high speed until light and fluffy, about two minutes, scraping the bowl as needed to incorporate all of the chocolate.

3 You can store any unused buttercream in the refrigerator in an airtight container; let it come to room temperature and then give it a quick whip in the mixer before using.

Tips and Tricks

If you do not have an icing tip, you can pipe on the frosting by scooping it into a plastic bag and snipping off the corner using scissors. Take a fork and poke around the frosting, making it look like hair. If the frosting is too thick, you can add a little more milk to get your desired consistency. You can attach the wafers onto pretzel sticks in place of the toothpicks if you would like everything to be edible. You can use a premade cake mix instead of homemade. If the box calls for 24 regular cupcakes you will get 12 large cupcakes.

Animal Fact

Brown bears are very powerful animals that live in the forests and mountains of North America, Europe, and Asia. They are the most common bears in the world and one of the largest of all the bear species. They like to feed on nuts, berries, fruit, leaves, roots, and sometimes small animals. Bears that live on the coast love to eat salmon. Bears will eat up to 90 pounds of food each day to prepare for winter. Bears dig dens for winter hibernation and will hibernate for five to eight months. Brown bears can live up to 25 years.

Cheetah Cheesecake

These cute cheesecakes are very easy to make, and your kids will think these are so cool! You can always add a drop or two of yellow food coloring to give them a brighter color, but we like the pale yellow that this recipe gives.

Ingredients

(makes 5-6 servings)

- 1 cup graham cracker crumbs
- 3 ½ tablespoons brown sugar
- ½ teaspoon ground cinnamon
- 3 ½ tablespoons butter, melted
- 1 (8-ounce) package of cream cheese (softened)
- 2 teaspoons of lemon juice
- 1 ⅓ cups heavy whipping cream
- 3 ½ tablespoons of white sugar
- marshmallows
- Tootsie Rolls
- mini chocolate chips
- chocolate chips
- mini vanilla wafers

Directions

. . . . . .

1 In a small bowl, stir together the graham cracker crumbs, brown sugar, and cinnamon. Add the melted butter and mix until completely blended. Press the mixture into five or six small brulée ramekins (5 inches in diameter) or any other small, round dish. Chill until firm.

2 In a medium bowl, beat together the cream cheese and lemon juice until blended. Add the whipping cream and beat with an electric mixer until the batter becomes thick. Add the sugar and continue to beat until stiff. Pour the cream cheese mixture into the chilled crust. Chill for a few hours before decorating.

3 Cut the tips off of the marshmallows using kitchen scissors and place them on the tops for eyes. Put a Tootsie Roll in the microwave for seven to eight seconds to soften and cut it in half. Shape the halves into noses and place on top of the cheesecake. Add mini chocolate chips for the mouth. Add regular chocolate chips for the pupils. Alternate the regular and mini chocolate chips around the face to look like spots. Add two mini vanilla wafers on the top sides for the ears.

Tips and Tricks

You can replace the chocolate chips with raisins and the Tootsie Roll nose with an almond for a healthier choice. You can also skip making the homemade recipe and purchase a box of no-bake cheesecake mix to make things easier.

Animal Fact

The cheetah is the world's fastest land animal. Their speed helps them pursue their prey, and they can go from zero to 60 miles an hour in just a few seconds. Cheetahs have black spots to help camouflage in their natural habitats. Cheetahs are carnivores, which means they only like to eat meat. Cheetahs only need to take a drink every three to four days. Most wild cheetahs are found in eastern and southwestern Africa. Cheetahs can live up to 10 to 12 years in the wild.

Animal Cupcake Cones

There is something about cupcake cones that the kids just love. Here are a few fun animal cupcake cone ideas that the kids will have fun decorating themselves using candies and sprinkles. We like to make a cake pop mixture to fill our cones instead of baking them. This way you can make them a day ahead for a party and they will stay crispy. If you bake the cake in the cone, sometimes the cones get really soggy.

Ingredients

(makes 6–8 cones)

- 1 box of cake mix (flavor of your choice)
- 1 can each of chocolate and vanilla frosting
- 1 box of colored ice cream cones (green, brown, and pink)
- large Tootsie Rolls
- mini marshmallows
- chocolate chips
- mini chocolate chips
- red sprinkles
- pink and green food coloring
- marshmallows
- red gumdrop
- pink wafers
- pink candy melts

Directions
• • • • • •

1 Preheat the oven to 350 degrees F. Mix the cake mix according to package directions. Bake in a 9x13-inch pan according to directions. When the cake is done baking, let it cool for about 20 minutes.

2 Break off pieces of the cake and place them in a bowl. Mash up the cake using a fork or electric mixer until completely broken up. Mix in ¾ can of chocolate frosting. Spoon the mixture into the ice cream cones.

3 To decorate the dog cone you will frost the top with the reserved chocolate frosting. Place a large Tootsie Roll in the microwave for seven to eight seconds and cut it in half. Shape the halves into ears using your fingers. Break a toothpick in half and poke the end into the ear. Poke the other end into the frosting and cake mixture to hold. Add a little frosting on the front of the cone for the mouth using a toothpick. Place on a chocolate chip for the nose. Cut a mini marshmallow in half for the eyes and use mini chocolate chips for the pupils, attaching with the frosting. Press on a red sprinkle under the mouth for a tongue.

4 To decorate the frog cone you will color the vanilla frosting using two drops of green food coloring. Frost the top of the cake mixture. Cut a marshmallow in half and place the halves on the top for the eyes. Add chocolate chips on top for the pupils. Add 2 mini chocolate chips on the top front for the nose. Cut a red gumdrop in strips using kitchen scissors and press the strips on the front for the mouth and tongue. Add a mini chocolate chip on the bottom of the tongue to look like a fly. Using a toothpick, you can add a little bit of the vanilla frosting on the sides of the mini chocolate chip to look like wings.

5 To decorate the pig cone, color the vanilla frosting with pink food coloring. Top the cake mixture with the pink frosting. Cut off pieces from pink wafers, shaping them into triangles, and place them on top for ears. Attach a pink candy melt to the front, topping with two mini chocolate chips using the frosting. Cut a mini marshmallow in half for the eyes and place two mini chocolate chips on top for the pupils using the frosting.

Tips and Tricks

If you decided to bake the cake in the cones instead of using the mixture, make sure you cover a muffin pan using aluminum foil to prevent the cones from tipping over. You can use any other candies you have on hand to decorate these, sticking with the same colors.

Monkey Banana Bread Cake Pops

You can create these fun monkey pops with a loaf of banana bread. These pops are a fun treat for the kids to help make. They like to smash the bread, mix it with the frosting, and shape it into balls. You will have to help them with the dipping and decorating, or your little monkeys might get a little messy in the kitchen!

Ingredients

- 1 loaf of banana bread (recipe to the right)
- 1 16-ounce container vanilla frosting
- 2 bags peanut butter chips
- 1 bag peanut butter cup minis
- 1 bag peanut butter cups (miniatures)
- candy eyes
- caramel bits
- lollipop sticks (decorative straws optional)

Banana Bread

- ⅓ cup milk
- 1 teaspoon vinegar
- 2 eggs, beaten
- ½ cup vegetable oil
- 2 ½ cups mashed bananas
- 1 ½ cups white sugar
- 1 ¾ cups all-purpose flour
- 1 teaspoon baking soda
- ½ teaspoon salt

Directions

• • • • • •

1 Preheat the oven to 325 degrees F. Spray one 9x5-inch loaf pan with cooking spray. Mix the milk and vinegar. Stir together the eggs, milk mixture, oil, and bananas until well blended. Sift together the sugar, flour, baking soda, and salt. Add to banana mixture. Pour into the prepared loaf pan and bake one hour and 15 minutes or until a cake tester inserted in the center comes out clean.

2 Once the bread has cooled, cut off pieces of it into a large bowl and mash using a fork or mixer. You can also use a blender. Mix in the container of vanilla frosting. Shape the mixture into 1 ½- to 2-inch balls and place them on a pan lined with wax paper. Place the cake balls in the fridge for about 30 minutes to one hour.

3 Melt the peanut butter chips in the microwave for 30 seconds and stir. Place back in the microwave for an additional 20 seconds at a time until melted. Do not overheat! Dip a lollipop stick in the melted chips and then push on a cake ball. Let that set for a few minutes.

4 Dip the banana cake pop back in the melted chips and cover. You can spread evenly using the back of a spoon. Place the covered balls in a tall glass or anything you have to set them up straight to set and harden.

5 Attach the peanut butter cup minis on the sides to look like ears. Place a miniature peanut butter cup on the front for the snout (you can cut them in half first so they do not stick out too much) and press on the candy eyes using the melted chips if needed. Shape the caramel bits by pressing with your fingers to make the nose, mouth, and inside of the ears.

6 Place the pops on decorative straws for extra color (if desired).

Tips and Tricks

You can use any cake mix flavor for this, if your kids do not prefer banana. Just follow the package directions and add the frosting after baking. You can pipe on melted peanut butter chips in place of the caramel bits. You can replace the milk and vinegar mixture by using buttermilk.

Animal Fact

Monkeys are found all over the world and come in several different colors, sizes, and shapes. There are over 250 species of monkeys. Monkeys like to live on the ground and in trees. Mandrills are the largest of all monkeys, and pygmy marmosets are known to be among the smallest of all monkeys. Spider monkeys get their names from having such long arms, legs, and tails. Even though monkeys are known to eat bananas, they mostly eat nuts, seeds, fruits, and flowers.

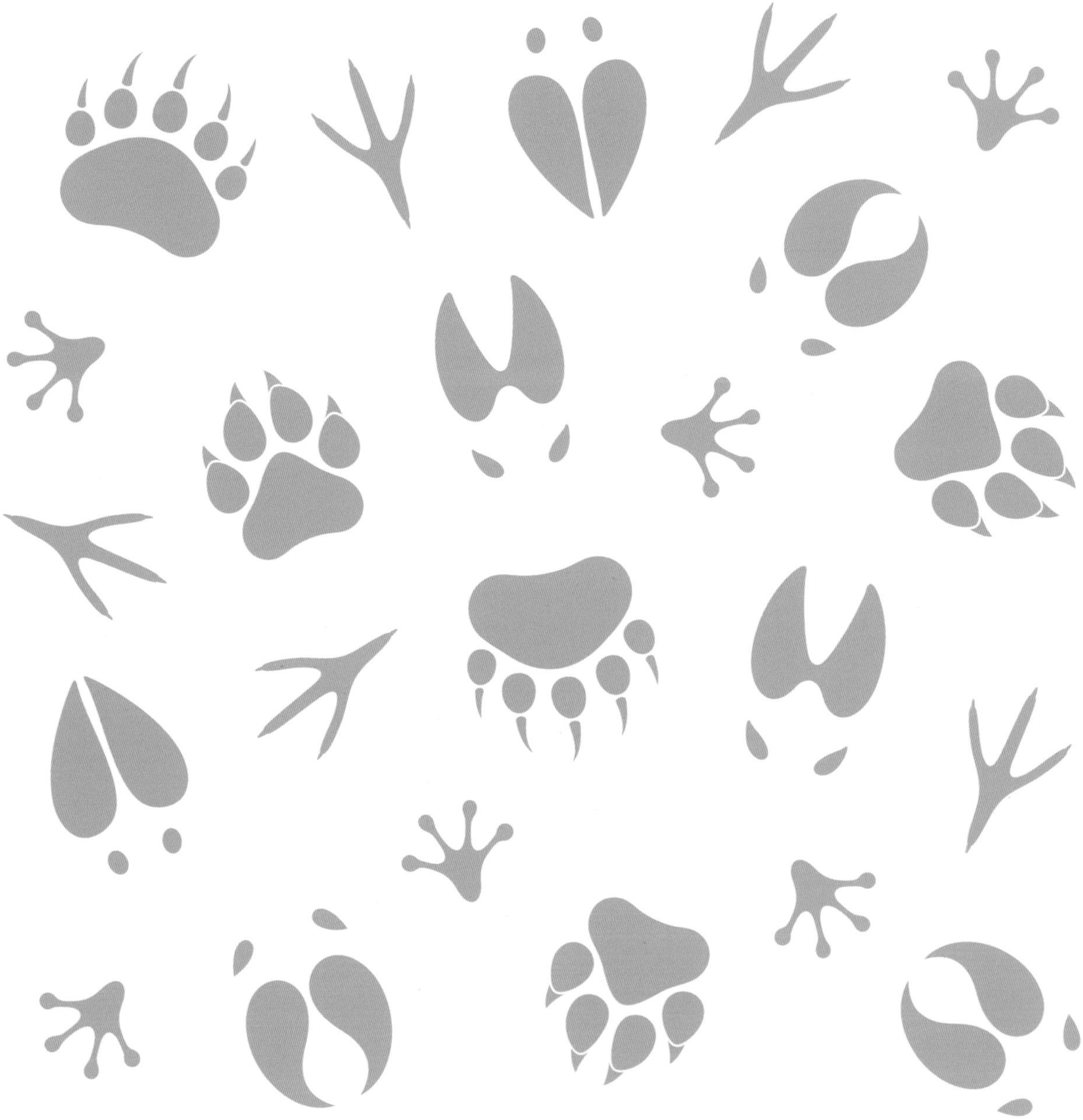

ACKNOWLEDGMENTS

I never dreamed that having some fun in the kitchen with my boys would turn into a successful blog that has also opened up so many new doors. If you would have told me years ago before I had kids that I would be creating fun food ideas, I would have laughed and said you are absolutely crazy! It is funny how changes in your life provide so many opportunities that you would have never thought of before (for instance, writing my first cookbook)! I feel so blessed that not only do I get to create lots of fun memories with my little boys, but I also get to inspire others to create in the kitchen, sharing those same special memories. All of this would not be possible without the blessings of my savior Jesus Christ.

I'd like to thank everyone who has visited KitchenFunWithMy3Sons.com throughout the years. Without you, this book would not be possible. This also includes those of you connecting with us on social media including Facebook, Pinterest, Instagram, Twitter, and Google Plus. Your comments and emails mean the world to us. We always look forward to all of your emails or comments, including pictures with your re-creations of our fun food ideas. We are so thankful for your support and encouragement that you give us daily.

I am so thankful for my three boys, Von, Dane, and Levi. None of this would exist without the three of you. Von, you are one of the most creative people I have ever met. You continuously blow me away with all of your ideas and art. You have been such a big part in helping come up with lots of our food ideas;

you also have such a great eye. Dane, you are the main reason we started our fun food creations and blog, because of your picky food choices as a toddler. You are definitely my most photogenic of the bunch, and you are such a great hands-on helper. Levi, you have always loved being my best kitchen helper and definitely are the one who loves to cook the most. You always drop anything that you are doing to run into the kitchen and help me create. You guys will never know the joy that you have given me, not only in making fun memories with you in the kitchen, but also in watching all of you grow into such amazing boys.

A big thank-you to my husband, Josh. For all the times that you waited on breakfast/dinner until the photos for this book were taken; for your patience while I endured late nights doing blog postings; for your help with the dishes, your artistic input, and your big appetite for all food no matter what it looks like; for putting up with the stress that comes along with writing a book; and for all of your support. You are my best friend, and this is all possible because of your love and encouragement.

Mom, you are the inspiration behind this fun food journey of ours. I have such happy memories of my fun birthday cakes that you took the time to create for me when I was a little girl. I can only hope to create those same wonderful memories with my boys. You are everything I want to be, and I can never thank you enough for all the times you have been there for me. I love you dearly. Brian, you are the best big brother anyone could have. You have helped me so much through this journey, and I will give you total credit on the "Oh No, the Turtle Turned Over" watermelon idea! Thank you for always being there for me. Our Penguin Soup is dedicated to you! Dad, you are my biggest fan. I am sure you are smiling down on me and bragging to everyone in heaven about me like you did while you were still here with us. I miss you every day and hope I still make you proud.

To my mother-in-law, Diane, who has liked every post we have ever put on Facebook. You have been so supportive of our blog from day one, and I greatly appreciate you. Thanks to my Aunt Debby for spending so much time helping and supporting me.

Thank you to all of my wonderful fun food blogger friends who have given me so much support and guidance. Thanks for all of your listening, advice, sharing our creations, commenting, answering my questions, and contributing to the success of our blog and this book. A special thanks to Meaghan Mountford, Beth Jackson Klosterboer, Norene Cox, Dorothy Kern, Amy Locurto, Sue Sparks, Amy Roskelley, Kim Heimbuck, Sandra Denneler, Alejandra Morin, Michelle Castenada, Mindy Cone, and Toni Miller.

To my editor Julie Ganz and the team at Skyhorse Publishing: Thank you for having faith in me to write this book and giving me this opportunity. A big thanks to Julie for answering my hundreds of questions and for all of your patience with me.

To my friends who have given me so much support—thank you! Gene, you are so gifted and have such rare talent. We are so lucky to have you for a friend and beyond grateful for your help with our blog, and through this whole book process. Erinn, you have always been so encouraging and helpful and such a dear friend. I love you! Erica, thank you for listening to me every day and being so supportive.

Finally, thank you for buying this book. I hope that you and your kids enjoy spending time together, getting crafty in the kitchen, discovering new and interesting animal facts, eating yummy food, and having a wild time in the kitchen!